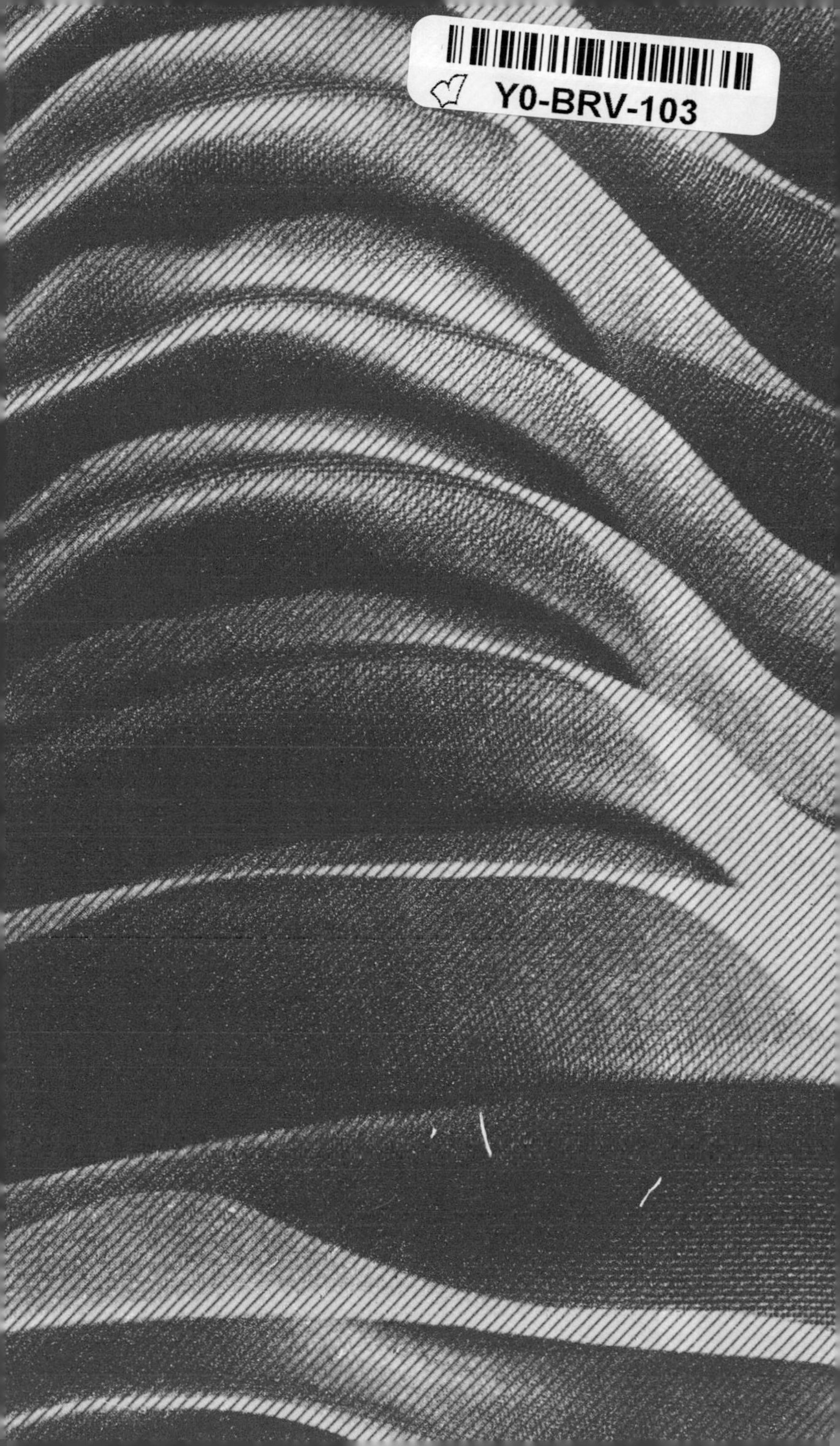
Y0-BRV-103

THE CENTRAL LENIN MUSEUM

Lenin. 1920.

THE CENTRAL LENIN MUSEUM

A GUIDE

RADUGA PUBLISHERS
MOSCOW

ЦЕНТРАЛЬНЫЙ МУЗЕЙ В. И. ЛЕНИНА

Путеводитель на английском языке

Редакция литературы по спорту и туризму

Compiled by V. I. DEVYATOV
A. Ye. KAZAKOV
O. S. KRIVOSHEINA
V. V. MICHUROV
I. N. NAZAROV
V. S. SHAKULOVA
L. I. SHEMYAKINA

Translated from the Russian by *Vyacheslav Semyonov*
Editor of the Russian text *Martha Derzhavina*
Editors of the English text *Alexandra Bouianovskaya* and *Alexander Kafyrov*
Designed by *Irina Markarova*
Art editor *Nina Shcherbakova*
Maps by *Lyubov Cheltsova*
Photos: The Central Lenin Museum
Layout by *Irina Dergunova* and *Galina Nemtinova*

Ц $\frac{1905040100\text{-}403}{031(05)\text{-}86}$ 061-86

ISBN 5-05-000692-9

GROUND FLOOR. Rooms Nos. 1-10

FIRST FLOOR. Rooms Nos. 11-23

LENIN

Millions of people pronounce his name with love and reverence. No other man in history has had so much influence on the life of entire nations and on the course of events throughout the world. No one evokes such vivid memories or such a degree of admiration. Lenin's teachings and deeds are alive today. He is remembered above all for his powerful mind, indomitable will, and revolutionary zeal. He was totally opposed to all forms of servitude, all oppression. He possessed a genuine talent for organizing the masses and had an inspired faith in the creative abilities of the proletariat.

It was under Lenin's leadership that Russia's workers and peasants took over power in 1917 and established the world's first socialist state; led by Lenin they later fought to defend Soviet power in the Civil War and laid the foundations of socialism in their country. His name was a rallying banner for the Soviet people who rose to defend what socialism had given them against the German onslaught in World War II. He is ever present in the hearts and minds of those who are today building Communism, a society whose motto is, "Everything for the sake of man, for the benefit of man."

Lenin's versatile genius is revealed in his books, articles and letters. Numerous documents, eye-witness accounts and the recollections of those who knew him bring him close to us.

We now invite you to follow us to the Lenin Museum in Moscow.

The Museum was first opened as a branch of the V. I. Lenin Institute in May 1924, and twelve years later it was set up on its own as the Central Lenin Museum. On its three floors there are 34 rooms with more than 12.5 thousand items on display, including first editions, photostats of manuscripts, photographs, personal possessions belonging to Lenin and presents he received. Among the exhibits are also paintings, drawings and sculpture.

All of Lenin's life and work is linked with the history of the Soviet Communist Party and of the world's first socialist state. On view, at the museum, are various exhibits telling the story of the 1917 Socialist Revolution in Russia, the Civil War, the Great Patriotic War of 1941-1945 against Nazi Germany, and the construction of a new social system in the USSR. There are other exhibits relating to the international revolutionary movement.

In the sixty years of its existence the Museum has been visited by more than fifty-five million people from over 100 countries.

The Central Lenin Museum. Revolution Square.

There are ten rooms on the ground floor where the exhibition starts, thirteen on the first, and eleven on the second. There are several escalators for the visitors' convenience.

On average a tour lasts two hours.

UNDER THE LENIN BANNER

COME AND HEAR

1

GROUND FLOOR

ROOMS NOS 1·10

РОССІЙСКАЯ СОЦІАЛЬ-ДЕМОКРАТИЧЕСКАЯ РАБОЧАЯ ПАРТІЯ

ИСКРА

№ 1. ДЕКАБРЬ 1900 ГОДА. № 1.

НАСУЩНЫЯ ЗАДАЧИ НАШЕГО ДВИЖЕНІЯ.

ВИЛЬГЕЛЬМЪ ЛИБКНЕХТЪ

The Socialist Revolution in Russia has found reflection in the fine arts abroad. Poster, one of the exhibits in the museum.

Vladimir Ulyanov, as a schoolboy. 1887.

CHILDHOOD AND ADOLESCENCE. EARLY REVOLUTIONARY ACTIVITIES. LENIN'S CONTRIBUTION TO THE EVOLUTION OF MARXISM (1870-1900)

Vladimir Ilyich Ulyanov (Lenin) was born on April 10 (22)[1], 1870 in the city of Simbirsk (now Ulyanovsk) on the Volga. Lenin came from a family with roots running deep into the heart of the Russian people. His grandfather, Nikolai Vasilyevich Ulyanov, of serf peasant stock, was himself a serf belonging to a landowner from Nizhni Novgorod (now Gorky) Province. At the end of the 18th century he went to work in the lower reaches of the Volga from whence he chose not to return to his master. He lived later in Astrakhan (a town in the mouth of the Volga), where for a time he was classified as a government peasant. Here he began to work as a tailor and was registered as belonging to the lower middle class. He died in dire poverty.

[1] Dates before January 31 (February 13), 1918 will be given according to the Julian calendar which was in use in Russia before that date.

Ilya Nikolayevich Ulyanov, Lenin's father.

Maria Alexandrovna Ulyanova, Lenin's mother.

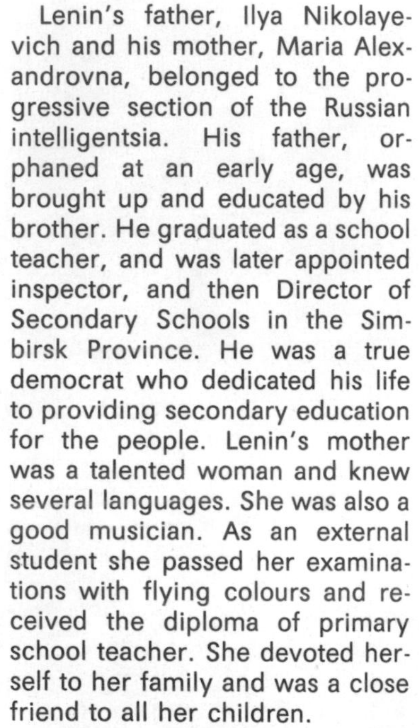

Lenin's father, Ilya Nikolayevich and his mother, Maria Alexandrovna, belonged to the progressive section of the Russian intelligentsia. His father, orphaned at an early age, was brought up and educated by his brother. He graduated as a school teacher, and was later appointed inspector, and then Director of Secondary Schools in the Simbirsk Province. He was a true democrat who dedicated his life to providing secondary education for the people. Lenin's mother was a talented woman and knew several languages. She was also a good musician. As an external student she passed her examinations with flying colours and received the diploma of primary school teacher. She devoted herself to her family and was a close friend to all her children.

Lenin's parents brought up their children to be honest, industrious, and considerate to others. They instilled in them a sense of responsibility for their words and actions, and a strong sense of duty. All the Ulyanov children, except Olga who died at an early age, became revolutionaries.

To the left of the entrance is a display of the Ulyanov family photographs. An 1879 photo shows Lenin's father and mother with their children—sons Alexander, Vladimir and Dmitri and daughters Anna, Maria and Olga. There is also a photo of Lenin's brother Alexander who was executed on May 8, 1887 for his part in the attempt on the life of Tsar Alexander III. It was from Alexander that Vladimir imbibed revolutionary and democratic ideas and learnt about Marxist literature, and it was Alexander who first showed his younger brother Karl Marx's *Das Kapital*.

On view here is a replica of Vladimir Ulyanov's room in the house in Simbirsk where his fam-

The Ulyanovs. Simbirsk. 1879.

ily lived between 1878 and 1887. The house (present address: 58, Ulitsa Lenina, Ulyanovsk) has been converted into a Lenin Memorial Museum. All that Vladimir's room contained was a desk by the window, a simple bookshelf, and a map of the world on the wall. One of the books on the shelf is *What Is To Be Done?* by the revolutionary democrat N. G. Chernyshevsky.

As a pupil of the Simbirsk Classical Gymnasium (there is a photo of the school in the room) Vladimir Ulyanov passed from one grade to the next with highest distinctions. He graduated from the school with a Gold Medal of Merit. A copy of this and other awards are to be seen in the first section of the display. A glass case contains books from the Ulyanovs' family library: Pushkin, Lermontov, Gogol, Turgenev, Lev Tolstoy, Hertzen, Dobrolyubov, Shakespeare, Darwin, and Huxley. Progressive literature had a tremendous influence on the Ulyanov children.

After the untimely death in January 1886 of Lenin's father, the family moved in the summer of 1887 to the city of Kazan where Vladimir became a student at the University. A photograph shows the University building and the University admission card No. 197 issued to V. I. Ulyanov, a student of the law department. The school report (on display) submitted to the University authorities by the principal of the Simbirsk Gymnasium reads as follows: "Ulyanov is highly talented, consistently hardworking and accurate. Each year he passed out top

Выпускъ III.

ЧТО ТАКОЕ „ДРУЗЬЯ НАРОДА"
и
КАКЪ ОНИ ВОЮЮТЪ ПРОТИВЪ
СОЦIАЛ - ДЕМОКРАТОВЪ.

Сентябрь 1894

Изданiе
провинцiальной группы
соцiал-демократовъ

Cover of *What the "Friends of the People" Are and How They Fight the Social-Democrats*. 1894 edition.

of his class, and on finishing school he was awarded a Gold Medal as a most deserving pupil for his studies, general erudition and behaviour ..."

At the University, Vladimir Ulyanov established contact with revolutionary-minded students. After being arrested in December 1887 as an active participant in a students' rally he was expelled from the University. He was banished to the village of Kokushkino some 40 kilometres from Kazan where he lived under police surveillance for nearly a year. While here he read widely and continued to work independently for his degree. Photographs show the village of Kokushkino and the Kazan Kremlin inside whose walls stood a prison to which Vladimir was confined after his arrest.

On his return to Kazan, Vladimir joined one of the underground Marxist societies organized by N. Ye. Fedoseyev whose photograph is displayed in the room. As a member of a Marxist society Lenin studied *Das Kapital*

ИЗДАНІЕ М. И. ВОДОВОЗОВОЙ.

Владиміръ Ильинъ.

РАЗВИТІЕ КАПИТАЛИЗМА

ВЪ РОССІИ.

Процессъ образованія внутренняго рынка для крупной промышленности.

Цѣна 2 р. 50 к.

С.-ПЕТЕРБУРГЪ.
Типо-литографія А. Лейферта, Бол. Морская, 65.
1899.

Cover of *The Development of Capitalism in Russia*. 1899 edition.

and other works by the founders of scientific communism. On view in a show-case are books by Karl Marx and Friedrich Engels translated into Russian by G. V. Plekhanov, an outstanding propagandist of Marxism in Russia and by other members of the Emancipation of Labour, a Russian Marxist group in Geneva. These were the works that the young Ulyanov read and studied in Kazan.

Early in May 1889 the Ulyanov family went to live on a farm near the village of Alakayevka in the Samara Province, moving in the autumn to the capital of the province Samara (now Kuibyshev). In Samara, where he lived for nearly four years, Vladimir became actively involved in revolutionary activities: he organized and led the first Marxist society in the city. He also read for his University degree. In a stand devoted to this period of Lenin's life the following items are to be seen: a photograph of the house, now the V. I. Lenin Museum, in which the Ulyanov family lived between 1889 and 1893; books on Russia's economy read by Lenin at the local library; and the manuscript of his 1893 article "New Economic Developments in Peasant Life", one of his earliest works to have come down to us. Among the exhibits in this room are works by Karl Marx and Friedrich Engels studied by members of the Marxist society organized by Lenin. It was while he was in Samara that Lenin translated from German into Russian "The Manifesto of the Communist Party" written by Marx and Engels in 1848, the first ever Communist programme. The manuscript of the translation, which has unfortunately been lost, was passed from one reader to another. It was studied by members of the revolutionary youth societies in Samara and other Volga-side cities.

Also on view are: V. I. Ulyanov's request to be allowed to sit exams for his University degree; the First Class Diploma issued to him in 1891 as an external graduate of the law department at St. Petersburg University; one of the first legal cases handled by Lenin as a barrister at the Samara District Court.

The years in Kazan and Samara were of great significance for Lenin's future revolutionary work. It was during this period that he became a convinced Marxist. However, life in the provinces could not satisfy Lenin. He hungered for large-scale revolutionary activities to be at the centre of the political struggle. On August 31, 1893 he left for St. Petersburg.

There is a wide selection of documentary material on display devoted to his life and revolutionary work in the capital which coincided with a massive upsurge of the working-class movement in various parts of Russia, particularly in St. Petersburg. Living in the capital of the Russian Empire, the hub of the working-class movement in Russia, he established contact with progressive-minded workers at major factories, lectured to Marxist groups and explained the most complex points of Marx's doctrine. Lenin had a profound knowledge of Marxism and was able to apply it in the conditions existing in Russia at the time. This, and his firm conviction that the revolutionary cause must win, as well as his outstanding ability as an organizer soon made him the acknowledged leader of the Marxists in St. Petersburg.

One stand is devoted to photographs of I. V. Babushkin, M. I. Kalinin, V. A. Shelgunov, V. A. Knyazev and other members of Lenin's Marxist study group. They were all workers and leaders of similar workers' study groups at factories and other industrial enterprises in St. Petersburg. There is a photograph here of Nadezhda Krupskaya, a young teacher at a Sunday evening school for workers, who engaged in propaganda work and spread Marxist ideas among her students. Lenin first met Nadezhda Krupskaya, whom he later married, at a secret Social-Democratic meeting. In St. Petersburg, Lenin was under constant police surveillance, and had to change his place of residence on many

Lenin and other leading members of the Petersburg League of Struggle for the Emancipation of the Working Class. February 1897.

occasions. The photographs on display show the houses where Lenin lived at the time or gave lectures.

Lenin was a vigorous opponent of anti-Marxist trends, such as Liberal Populism* and Legal Marxism* which hindered the dissemination of Marxism in Russia. Occupying the central place in a display stand is the first hectograph edition of *What the "Friends of the People" Are and How They Fight the Social-Democrats* (1894). In this pamphlet the 24-year-old Lenin set forth the major tenets of the revolutionary Social-Democrat programme; the role of the working class in Russia as the leading force in a future revolution; the need for an alliance of workers and peasants as the basic condition for the overthrow of the Tsarist regime, the need to create a Marxist working-class party and its leading role in the fight for democracy and socialism. The pamphlet was printed in Moscow, St. Petersburg and in some other places.

In October 1895 a number of separate Marxist groups and societies in St. Petersburg were united under Lenin's guidance into a single Social-Democratic organization which in December that year became known as the League of Struggle for the Emancipation of the Working Class. The League was to become the embryo of a revolutionary party of the Russian proletariat. It linked the workers' demands for higher pay and better working conditions with the political struggle against the Tsarist regime and capitalist exploitation. In the upper part of the display on the wall opposite the entrance, is an enlarged photograph showing some of the League's leaders, with Lenin in the centre. A diagram shows the structure of the League and the links it maintained with similar organizations in other Russian cities. Next to it are photographs of members of a Social-Democratic organization, the Moscow Workers' League among whom we find Lenin's younger brother and sister, Dmitri and Maria.

At this time, the St. Petersburg League switched over from Marxist propaganda conducted within the narrow confines of workers' societies to a campaign of political agitation among the working masses at large. It led the strike movement of workers in St. Petersburg, printed and distributed leaflets, pamphlets and other literature, much of it written by Lenin. Some of that literature is to be seen in the stand devoted to the period.

In the spring of 1895 Lenin went abroad to establish contact with the Russian Marxists living there and to learn from the experience of the West-European revolutionaries. In Geneva, Paris and Berlin he attended meetings of workers and studied the conditions of their life. He met the revolutionary leader Paul Lafargue and one of the German Social-Democratic leaders Wilhelm Liebknecht. At public libraries he read Marxist literature not available in Russia, copying out whole passages and making synopses of

* See Notes at the end of the book.

Lenin. 1891.

some of the books. On display is the synopsis Lenin made of Part One of Gustave Lefrançais' *Etude sur le mouvement communaliste à Paris, en 1871*, plus letters he wrote from Paris and Berlin to relatives.

Lenin returned to Russia early in September 1895. He immediately became the target of close police surveillance and was finally arrested in December that year. For 14 months before his trial he was held in solitary confinement in Cell No. 193 (a photograph of the cell is on view) in a St. Petersburg prison. Lenin kept up his revolutionary work even in prison. Establishing contact with those of his comrades who were still at liberty, he continued through them to guide the League. "The Draft and Explanation of a Programme for the Social-Democratic Party" and a leaflet, "To the Tsarist Government", written by Lenin in jail, form part of the display. These and other illegal works were written with lemon juice or milk which he poured into improvised ink-wells made out of bread.

In February 1897 Lenin was sentenced to three years of exile in Eastern Siberia. He served his term in the village of Shushenskoye, Yenisei Province. At the turn of the century Shushenskoye

Nadezhda Krupskaya. 1895.

was a remote place, the nearest railway being hundreds of kilometres away. Today, it is a regional centre of the Krasnoyarsk Territory. In 1938 a Lenin House-Museum was opened in the village. The adjoining streets and houses, restored to look as they did at the end of the 19th century, have been declared a protected area. In the stand dedicated to Lenin's Siberian exile there is a photograph of the house, belonging to Zyryanov, one of the villagers with whom Lenin lodged on his arrival from St. Petersburg. By the wall on the right stands a scale model of the house—owned by Petrova, another villager—where Lenin lived with Nadezhda Krupskaya and her mother, following their arrival at Shushenskoye, in May 1898. Here Nadezhda Krupskaya, who had also been sentenced to exile in Shushenskoye by the court which had tried the League's case in St. Petersburg, became Lenin's wife. She was to remain his close friend and loyal assistant for the rest of his life.

In exile, Lenin wrote some thirty theoretical papers in which he elaborated on many of the issues involved in working out a programme, strategy and tactics for a working-class party in Russia. He also completed *The De-*

The village of Shushenskoye at the beginning of the 20th century.

velopment of Capitalism in Russia, a direct sequel of *Das Kapital. The Development of Capitalism in Russia* is based on Lenin's knowledge of life and his studies of hundreds of books and statistics. Though there are over 600 literary sources mentioned and quoted in the book, Lenin in fact read and made use of many times that number of works. In *The Development of Capitalism* he argues that capitalism had been developing in Russia both in industry and in agriculture. He reveals the profound contradictions inherent in capitalist society and maintains that the Russian proletariat was a real force which could play a leading role in the Russian revolutionary movement. The book first appeared in St. Petersburg in March 1899 under one of Lenin's pseudonyms, Vladimir Ilyin.

Living in exile, Lenin often reread Marx and Engels, especially their philosophical works. He was an avid reader of the Russian and foreign press and followed every development in the Russian and international Social-Democratic movement. He continued his research on agrarian relations in Russia, studied rural life in Siberia, translated foreign publications into Russian and reviewed books. The exhibits relating to this period include his translations of *Industrial Democracy* by the English economists, Sidney and Beatrice Webb, his review of *The Evolution of Modern Capitalism* by the English economist J. A. Hobson published in the magazine *Nachalo* (The Beginning) (May 1899) and some other works.

Other exhibits in the room include the proceedings of the First Congress of the RSDLP* held in March 1898. The Congress, which failed to unite individual Social-Democratic groups in Russia, succeeded in officially proclaiming the foundation of the RSDLP. In Shushenskoye Lenin concentrated on devising ways to establish a united party. In a stand on the right are Lenin's articles, "Our Programme", "Our Immediate Tasks", and "An Urgent Question" in which he outlines a plan for creating a revolutionary working-class party with the help of an illegal national political newspaper.

At that time there were two other Social-Democratic exiles in Shushenskoye: O. A. Enberg, a

Finn, and a Pole, I. Prominski, both of them from the working class. And elsewhere in the district Lenin's revolutionary comrades from St. Petersburg, among them G. M. Krzhizhanovsky, A. A. Vaneyev, P. N. Lepeshinsky, V. V. Starkov, M. A. Silvin, V. K. Kurnatovsky, and others, were also serving terms of exile. Their photographs are to be seen in this room. Lenin used to meet them to discuss revolutionary work and to help them keep up their spirit. In August 1899 he wrote "The Protest of the Russian Social-Democrats", also on display in this room. The Protest was an uncompromising challenge to the Russian opportunist leaders, the Economists*, who maintained that the workers in Russia should confine themselves to the fight for better conditions, leaving the political struggle to the bourgeoisie. The Protest was signed by 17 political exiles who supported Lenin.

After a hard bout of work, Lenin used to retire to the forests, fields, or the river. He got to love Siberia's natural scenery and the deep Yenisei. The villagers in Shushenskoye still point out to visitors the steep river bank where he used to sit and admire the sunsets. A number of photographs in the display show some of Lenin's favourite haunts near the village: Crane and Sand Hills, Birch Copse, and Perovo Lake. At the end of the room are the table and two chairs used by Lenin and his wife in Petrova's house.

When Lenin's term of exile drew to an end, the government barred him from living in the capital, in industrial cities or university towns. He decided to go to Pskov, which was at the time a small provincial town not far from St. Petersburg. On January 29, 1900 Lenin and his wife left Shushenskoye. On his way to Pskov Lenin visited a number of towns (they are shown on the map in the last stand) to rally support from local Social-Democrats for the newspaper he planned to publish. In the same stand is a photograph of the house in Pskov (now a Lenin House-Museum) where a meeting chaired by Lenin was held to discuss his draft declaration on behalf of the editorial board of the newspaper. As police persecution made it impossible to produce a revolutionary newspaper in Russia, in July 1900 Lenin went abroad to put his plan into practice. This was Lenin's first period of emigration. It lasted almost 5 years—until November 1905.

TOWARDS A NEW TYPE OF MARXIST PARTY (1900-1904)

Early in the 20th century Russia was the scene of a growing revolutionary movement led by the working class. There was an increasing number of strikes at factories and plants, peasants revolted against their landowners, and there was unrest among students. This situation is illustrated by the map, "An Upsurge in the Revolutionary Movement in Russia, 1900-1903" and a photograph of striking workers in Rostov in 1902 which start off the display to the left of the room's entrance.

Abroad, Lenin worked hard to get his newspaper off the ground. He had to find premises for the printing press, buy sets of Russian type, devise a system for secret delivery of the newspaper to Russia, etc. His brainchild, the first Russian clandestine political newspaper was called *Iskra* (The Spark). In one of the first stands to the left there is a display of photographs of *Iskra*'s editorial staff: V. I. Lenin, G. V. Plekhanov,

V.I. Zasulich, P.B. Axelrod, L. Martov, and A. N. Potresov. In April 1901 Nadezhda Krupskaya joined the editorial board as a secretary. A leaflet (in the same stand) released by the paper's editors stresses that "Russian Social-Democrats must unite and direct all our efforts towards the formation of a strong party which must struggle under the single banner of revolutionary Social-Democracy". Lenin was *Iskra*'s ideological leader. He did the lay-out for each issue, edited the articles, enlisted contributors, kept in touch with the newspaper's correspondents, was in charge of financial matters, and ensured *Iskra*'s regular publication.

In 1900-1901 Lenin lived at 53a Kaiserstrasse in Munich, first illegally, without a passport, under the name of Meyer, and later, on a passport made out in the name of a Bulgarian Doctor Jordan Jordanov. A photograph of the house (now No. 46) is on view. For reasons of secrecy Lenin sent all his letters to Russia via Prague to the address of the Czech Social-Democrat, F. Modráček. Lenin was given much help in preparing for the publication of *Iskra* by the German and international working-class leader Clara Zetkin, by her compatriot the Social-Democrat Adolf Braun, and by the Polish revolutionary Julian Marchlewski whose photographs are on display. The exhibit in the middle of the left wall of the room is an authentic page from the first issue of *Iskra* with Lenin's editorial, "The Urgent Tasks of Our Movement". The first issue was printed in December 1900 at 48 Russenstrasse in Leipzig at the printing press owned by the German Social-Democrat H. Rau who published a small sports newspaper for workers. *Iskra*'s second and subsequent issues were printed at M. Ernst's printing press at 4 Söhnefelderstrasse (see a photograph on display) in Munich.

Iskra No. 4 (a copy of it can be seen in the stand to the right of the first issue) carries an article, "Where to Begin" in which Lenin describes the role a Russian national political newspaper could play in his plan for a new type of Marxist party in Russia. "A newspaper is not only a collective propagandist and a collective agitator," he wrote, "it is also a collective organiser." This was to become a basic principle of all subsequent Marxist publications. Displayed next to the copy of *Iskra* No. 4 is the political and scientific journal, *Zarya* (The Dawn), also published by the *Iskra* editorial board. It was in a double issue of this journal (Nos. 2-3) that the first four chapters of "The Agrarian Question and the 'Critics of Marxism'" appeared under the pseudonym "Lenin",[1] the first time that Lenin was to use this signature in print.

A wall album mounted to the left of *Iskra*'s first issue contains several articles that Lenin contributed to the paper on the main issues involved in setting up a Marxist party and in the class struggle of the proletariat. He

[1] For purposes of secrecy Lenin used over 160 pseudonyms.

Vladimir Ulyanov. 1900.

condemns the Tsarist regime and its reactionary policy, castigates the bourgeois liberals, exposes the nationalists, the anarchists and the Socialist Revolutionaries*, and levels sharp criticism at the Russian Economists with their opportunist policies. All in all, *Iskra* printed sixty of his articles.

In Russia and abroad Lenin established a number of *Iskra* promotion groups and a network of *Iskra* agents. A stand to the right displays photographs of the professional revolutionaries, Ivan Babushkin, Nikolai Bauman, Rozalia Zemlyachka, Mikhail Kalinin, Gleb Krzhizhanovsky and others who were *Iskra* agents. In spite of constant harassment from the secret police they supplied *Iskra* with material, organized delivery of the paper across the Russian border, and the collection of funds to keep it going.

Between April 1902 and April 1903 Lenin and his wife lived in London to where the paper had been moved from Munich. *Iskra*'s office was at 37a Clerkenwell-Green where the British Social-Democratic weekly *Justice* had its editorial office and whose press was used for printing *Iskra*. There is a photo of No. 37a on view.

In London, Lenin and his wife, who assumed the name of Richter, lived at first in furnished rooms. They later rented two small rooms near the British Museum in whose library Lenin often worked. He attended numerous meetings, studied the working-class movement in England, and improved his English. In the right-hand corner of the room there is a photograph of the building at 30 Holford Square where Lenin lived from 1902-1903. The mantelpiece and a piece of the wallpaper from his flat here is also on display.

Lenin's *Iskra* was delivered to Russia via London, Stockholm, Geneva, Marseilles, Vienna, Prague, Varna, and some other European cities. Its agents were German, Austrian, Czech, Swedish, and Bulgarian Social-Democrats. In a show-case in the left corner of the room are various objects used by those who smuggled *Iskra* into Russia—a suitcase with a false bottom, a specially tailored waistcoat, a roll of paper, and a set of children's bricks. Some copies of *Iskra* were reprinted at secret presses in Russia. A photograph shows one of these presses in Kishinev, Moldavia. Another exhibit is a scale model of a printing press in Baku, Azerbaijan, known to the Russian revolutionaries as Nina. On display is the matrix of an *Iskra* edition smuggled into Russia from Geneva, and a shelf fitted with a secret box in which *Iskra* was kept by the Ulyanov family.

It was during this period that Lenin wrote "What Is To Be Done? Burning Questions of Our Movement", a theoretical article which was largely instrumental in creating a revolutionary party of the Russian working-class. Occupying pride of place in an adjacent display case is a copy of the first edition of this book published in March 1902 in Stuttgart and sent into Russia secretly. Copies of it were discovered by the police during their searches

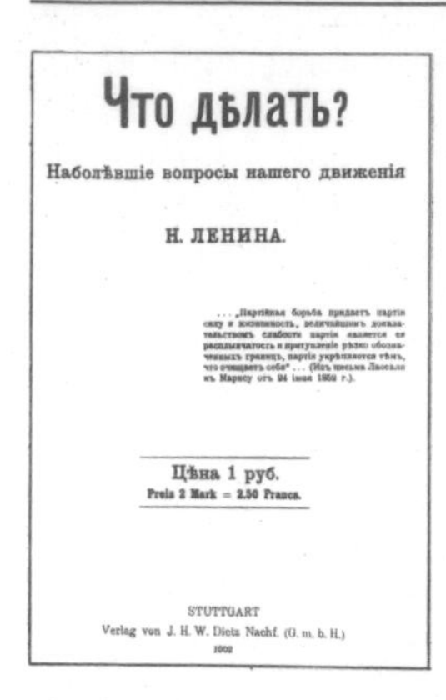

Что дѣлать?

Наболѣвшіе вопросы нашего движенія

Н. ЛЕНИНА.

. . . „Партійная борьба придаетъ партіи силу и жизненность, величайшимъ доказательствомъ слабости партіи является ея расплывчатость и притупленіе рѣзко обозначенныхъ границъ, партія укрѣпляется тѣмъ, что очищаетъ себя" . . . (Изъ письма Лассаля къ Марксу отъ 24 іюня 1852 г.).

Цѣна 1 руб.
Preis 2 Mark = 2.50 Francs.

STUTTGART
Verlag von J. H. W. Dietz Nachf. (G. m. b. H.)
1902

Cover of *What Is To Be Done? Burning Questions of Our Movement.* 1902 edition.

The British Museum's Reading Room in London where Lenin spent many hours.

and arrests of revolutionary workers in Moscow, St. Petersburg, Kiev, Nizhny Novgorod, Kazan, Odessa and other towns. Flanking the first edition are translations of it. In "What Is To Be Done?" Lenin denounces international opportunism and its Russian form, Economism. He also sets forth his basic ideas for a Marxist party as the leading force in the working-class movement and the transformation of existing society, and gives a detailed plan for the setting up of a militant, revolutionary party. "Give us an organization of revolutionaries, and we will overturn Russia!" he writes.

In a stand to the right of the entrance are the manuscripts for "Notes on Plekhanov's Second Draft Programme" and "The Agrarian Programme of Russian Social-Democracy" as well as a copy of *Iskra* No. 21 which carries the complete text of a draft of the party's programme drawn up by the paper's editors and incorporating Lenin's remarks and suggestions.

Another exhibit is a copy of *Iskra* No. 44 containing the article "The National Question in Our Programme" in which Lenin formulates the basic principles of a national programme for the revolutionary Social-Democrats in Russia. In March and April 1903, while still in London, he wrote *To the Rural Poor*, a pamphlet addressed to peasants in which he explains the aims of a revolutionary Social-Democratic party and why the rural poor should join the workers in their struggle. This pamphlet is among the exhibits in the stand.

Lenin placed great emphasis on propaganda of the Party's agrarian programme. He wrote a number of papers and delivered lectures on the subject in Paris, Lausanne, Geneva, Berne, Zurich, London, and Liege. In February 1903 he gave four lectures to students at the Russian Higher School of Social Sciences in Paris on the theme, "Marxist Views on the Agrarian Question in Europe and in Russia". A photocopy of

The printing shop in Leipzig where the first issue of *Iskra* came out.

the poster announcing these lectures is also exhibited in this room.

In the spring of 1903 the editorial offices of *Iskra* were transferred to Geneva. Lenin and his wife moved here from London, and rented a small house in Sécheron, a working-class suburb of the town. Here Lenin often met Russian revolutionaries who had left Russia after escaping from internal exile or prison. He used to spend hours talking to them and tried to help them as much as he could. Of an evening, Lenin's comrades would gather at his house to sing revolutionary songs like *the Internationale,* the *Marseillaise,* and the *Varshavianka.* Lenin who enjoyed singing would join in.

Lenin continued to edit *Iskra* which was printed by the General Workers' Printing Press at 27 de la Coulouvrenière. The collection of photographs in this room are of places connected with Lenin's life and work abroad from 1900-1903.

The last items on display in Rooms 2-3 relate to *Iskra*'s organization in Russia where the paper served as the ideological and organizational centre of revolutionary Social-Democracy in the country. This centre was created according to a plan drawn up by Lenin.

The last stand features a copy of the first edition of Lenin's pamphlet, *A Letter to a Comrade on Our Organisational Tasks.* Written in September 1902 it is a detailed account of the principles for the establishment of a revolutionary party to lead the working class to victory in its fight for political power.

* * *

Mounted in the corridor between Rooms 2 and 3 is a replica of the printing press in Leipzig where *Iskra*'s first issue was printed. It was presented as a gift to the Central Committee of the

Soviet Communist Party to mark the 50th anniversary of the 1917 October Revolution in Russia by the Central Committee of the Socialist Unity Party of Germany.

"As a current of political thought and as a political party, Bolshevism has existed since 1903." This quotation from Lenin in Room 3 introduces the main theme of the exhibition: the emergence of a party of the working class in Russia and the Second Congress of the Russian Social-Democratic Labour Party (RSDLP).

Lenin made thorough preparations for the Congress. He drew up Draft Rules for the Party, wrote an outline for his report on the *Iskra* organization's activities, and prepared other materials. He also worked out procedure for Congress meetings, its agenda, time limits for speakers and draft resolutions on the following subjects: workers' demonstrations, political work among the peasantry and servicemen, and attitude to students–the above items start off the display in this room.

The Congress which began on July 17, 1903 was held in a warehouse in a working-class suburb of Brussels. However, after the first session, interference from the Belgian police forced delegates to move to London. A map to the left of the entrance shows the 26 organizations which sent delegates to the Congress. Apart from the hard core of consistent revolutionaries fighting for the cause of the proletariat, the Congress was attended by the Economists, the Centrists* and other opportunistic leaders. This made the debates on many issues particularly heated and intense. Photographs on the wall show the delegates who supported Lenin. Two diagrams indicate the political alignment of forces at the Congress and the final results of the voting on key resolutions.

The Congress elected Lenin as its vice-chairman, and a member of the commissions which were to work out the Programme and Rules. He was also elected to the Credentials Committee. Rallying support for his views, Lenin made more than 130 speeches and critical comments. Among the exhibits are the following items: Lenin's manuscripts on the Party Programme and Rules; records of the speeches he made during the debate on these two issues; and separate sheets of paper with the numerous notes he jotted down as he listened to his opponents and supporters.

Some of the pages from his note pad have been incorporated into an album, *Lenin's Work at the Second Congress of the RSDLP*, also on view in this Room. A painting by Yu. Vinogradov *The Second Congress of the RSDLP*, portrays Lenin addressing delegates.

The Congress approved the Party Programme as drawn up by the *Iskra* editors who consistently followed the revolutionary course outlined by Marx and Engels. This is the first time in the history of the international working-class movement since the death of Marx and Engels that a revolutionary programme had been adopted proclaiming the dictatorship of the proletariat to be the principal goal of the working class. The Programme of the RSDLP stipulated that the proletariat's role was to lead all toiling and exploited masses in their fight for democracy and socialism. It also spoke of the peasants as allies of the working class. On display is a photocopy of the title page of one of the first editions of the Programme.

Among the other documents to be seen in this Room is Lenin's manuscript for the first paragraph of the draft for the Party Rules which demands that every member take part in the revolutionary struggle and obey party discipline. A note (a copy of it is on view) made by Lenin during the discussion of the Rules, reads as follows: "... the distinction between those who merely talk and those who work: it is better not to name as members ten workers than name one chatterer." Paragraph One of the Rules as formulated by Lenin barred Party membership to non-proletarian, vacillating, and opportunistic elements, thus making it possible to set up a strong, well-organized party with a strict discipline. This paragraph was the target of furious attacks from the opportunists.

In the elections for the Central Committee and for the Editorial Board of the Central Organ, the Party's two leading bodies, Lenin's supporters received a majority, or *bolshinstvo* of votes, and from then on became known as *bolsheviki*, the Bolsheviks. The opportunistic leaders who were left in the minority, or *menshinstvo*, were henceforth called *mensheviki*, the Mensheviks.

The conflict at the Congress

was frank and uncompromising. This is how Lenin himself described a few years afterwards a conversation he had had with a delegate representing the Centre. "'How oppressive the atmosphere is at our Congress!' he complained. 'This bitter fighting, this agitation one against the other, this biting controversy, this uncomradely attitude! ...' 'What a splendid thing our Congress is!' I replied. 'A free and open struggle. Opinions have been stated. The shades have been revealed. The groups have taken shape. Hands have been raised. A decision has been taken. A stage has been passed. Forward! That's the stuff for me! That's life! That's not like the endless, tedious word-chopping of your intellectuals, which stops not because the question has been settled, but because they are tired to talk any more ...'"

"The comrade of the 'Centre' stared at me in perplexity and shrugged his shoulders. We were talking different languages."

The Congress ended in complete victory for the revolutionary trend, became a turning point in the international working-class movement. It set up a new type of proletarian party capable of leading the industrial workers and other toiling masses in their fight to overthrow the rule of landowners and capitalists and build socialism.

After the Congress closed on August 10, 1903 Lenin and his supporters visited Karl Marx's grave at Highgate Cemetery. This event is portrayed in a drawing by A. Moravov.

N. LENIN. Ein Schritt vorwärts, zwei Schritt rückwärts
(Über die Krise in unserer Partei).

Россiйская Соцiальдемократическая Рабочая Партiя.

Н. ЛЕНИНЪ.

Шагъ впередъ,
два шага назадъ

(Кризисъ въ нашей Партiи)

ЖЕНЕВА
Типографiя Партiи. Rue de la Coulouvreniere. 27.
1904

Cover of *One Step Forward, Two Steps Back*. 1904 edition.

The Congress attracted the attention of the West-European Social-Democratic parties. Many newspapers and other publications gave detailed accounts of its proceedings and praised what it had achieved. In a stand are photocopies of pages from the Social-Democratic newspapers *Justice*, *Vorwärts* and others containing reports and commentary on the work of the Congress.

Here also are materials that reflect Lenin's battle with the Mensheviks after the Congress as well as resolutions and letters from local party committees in various Russian cities in support of the decisions taken at the Second Congress. Defeated at the Congress, the Mensheviks spared no efforts in their attempts to foil the implementation of the Congress decisions and to destabilize the work of the Party. They managed to get control of *Iskra* and the Party's Central Committee, publishing facilities, communication links and Party finances. They also attempted to spread their opportunistic influence to local party branches most of which supported Lenin and the Bolsheviks. This brought the Bolsheviks face to face with the problem of how to expose the Mensheviks as working against the Party.

Lenin tackled this problem in *One Step Forward, Two Steps Back (The Crisis in Our Party)* published in May 1904, in Geneva. The first Russian edition of this book, together with translations of it, is displayed on the right wall. In *One Step Forward, Two Steps Back,* Lenin denounces the Mensheviks as opportunists. He shows that the division into a majority and a minority at the Congress was a direct and inevitable consequence of the split between revolutionaries and opportunists that had long existed in other Social-Democratic parties. He develops in greater depth the Marxist doctrine on the party as a leading organization of the proletariat without which the victory of a socialist revolution and the building of a communist society are inconceivable. He also sets forth the Bolshevik organizational principles, firm standards of party life and principles of party leadership, all of which were from then on to be strictly observed by the party. A map to the right of the entrance illustrates the extensive links and correspondence which Lenin maintained with local party committees after the Congress (at the time he received up to three hundred letters a month). It shows that *One Step Forward* was read over a wide area in Russia.

In Switzerland, Lenin continued to work hard. While in Geneva in 1903-1904 he often made use of the University library. One of the chairs from the library, presented to the Museum by the city of Geneva, is on view in this room. Here also is a chess table with a secret drawer in which party documents and letters were kept. The table was made to Lenin's design.

The bitter struggle against the Mensheviks could not but undermine Lenin's health. He felt over-

Café Landolt in Geneva where Lenin used to meet Social-Democrats from Russia.

Chess-board table with a secret drawer in which documents of the Second RSDLP Congress were hidden.

worked and suffered from insomnia. Extreme exhaustion forced him to take a break. With his wife, Nadezhda Krupskaya, he spent a week in Lausanne, from there, rucksacks on their backs, they took off for a walking tour in the Alps.

For a short while after their hike they stayed in a small village near Lausanne. Here Lenin worked in the garden helping his host. Work in the open air which Lenin greatly enjoyed proved to be the best kind of rest cure. In the village, Lenin also met his party colleagues to discuss plans for the future.

In August 1904, 22 Bolsheviks held a conference presided over by Lenin in the Lausanne suburb of Carouge. They adopted an appeal "To the Party", written by Lenin, calling for the immediate convocation of the Third RSDLP Congress in order to rid the Party of the crisis caused by the Mensheviks' factionalist and destabilizing activities. On the wall is a photograph showing a general view of Carouge.

In their struggle against the Mensheviks, and their efforts to convene the Third Party Congress the Bolsheviks relied on their new newspaper, *Vperyod* (Forward). Founded by Lenin, it revived the revolutionary traditions of the Leninist *Iskra*. The latter paper (as from issue number 52) had fallen into the hands of the Mensheviks, who launched on its pages a vicious campaign against Lenin and the Bolsheviks. The first issue of *Vperyod*, printed in Geneva, is on display together with an advertisement announcing that it was about to appear, and with a photograph of the editors. Early in December 1904, Lenin delivered a series of lectures in Paris and some Swiss cities on the situation within the RSDLP. The money collected at these lectures was used to finance the publication of *Vperyod*.

The exhibition closes with a stand containing Lenin's letters to local party organizations and a number of party committee resolutions in support of his proposal for the convocation of a third Congress of the RSDLP.

Room No. 4

THE RUSSIAN REVOLUTION OF 1905-1907

Early on the morning of Sunday, January 9, 1905, a peaceful procession of workers from St. Petersburg factories marched slowly towards the Tsar's residence, the Winter Palace. Carrying church banners, icons and portraits of the Tsar, they intended to present him with a petition asking him to relieve their sufferings. Many of the 140 thousand marchers brought along their wives and children. Outside the Palace they were met by a line of soldiers, who, following the Tsar's orders, opened fire, killing more than one thousand unarmed petitioners and wounding another five thousand. A painting by I. Vladimirov depicting the massacre opens the display.

"Bloody Sunday" as this day became known, shook the entire country, triggering off a revolution. A collection of photographs showing the mass rallies and protest demonstrations that took place in major Russian cities in response to the massacre in Petersburg as well as leaflets calling for the overthrow of the autocratic regime and for an armed uprising, are on view.

From Geneva Lenin kept a close watch over developments in Russia and immediately responded to them. Among the exhibits is a copy of Issue No. 4 of the Bolshevik newspaper *Vperyod* which carried Lenin's article, "The Beginning of the Revolution in Russia". In it he emphasizes that on January 9, 1905 the working class had been taught a lesson in civil war, "the revolutionary education of the proletariat made more progress in one day than it could have made in months and years of drab, humdrum, wretched existence". Next to the newspaper is the manuscript of another article by Lenin, "New Tasks and New Forces", in which he sets forth the Party's tasks following the outbreak of the revolution. He wrote that in order to overthrow the tsarist autocracy the Party must mobilize and unite the proletariat in preparation for an armed uprising.

Cobble-stone, Weapon of the Proletariat.
Sculptor I. Shadr, 1927.

Lenin considered it was important to study the masses' experience of armed action. He read and carefully analyzed what Marx and Engels had written on the subject of revolutions. He was particularly interested in the Paris Commune and urged the Russian Social-Democrats and progressive revolutionary-minded workers to study its experience. In March 1905 he read a lecture on the Paris Commune at a gathering of the Russian political émigré colony in Geneva. An outline of the lecture is to be seen in one of the first stands in the room.

Lenin foresaw that the revolution would inevitably gain momentum. This being so, the Party had to decide on what line to take and on its tactics. This could only be done at a party congress. Several stands are devoted to Lenin's preparations for a third RSDLP Congress: two manuscripts "A Letter to Party Organizations in Russia" and "A Letter to the Zurich Group of Bolsheviks", and an editorial note to the "Report on the Third Congress of the Russian Social-Democratic Labour Party" in which he lists the main points to be discussed at the Congress.

The Third Congress was held between April 12 and 27, 1905 in London. Lenin took an active part in the proceedings. He had drawn up a strategic plan and had worked out the tactics to be followed by the Party in a bourgeois-democratic revolution. Under this plan, the Russian proletariat, allied with the peasantry, was to isolate the liberal bourgeoisie and bring off a bourgeois-democratic revolution. Its complete victory would clear the way for a socialist revolution. Photographs show the Bolshevik delegates at the Congress. Also on display are drafts of the main resolutions devised by Lenin: on an armed uprising, on a provisional revolutionary government, and on support for the peasants' movement. Having decided that the organization of an armed uprising was a task of top priority for the Party, the Congress instructed all party organizations to take steps to arm the proletariat, and to work out a plan for, and lead, an armed uprising.

Displayed left of the entrance is the first edition of *Two Tactics of Social-Democracy in the Democratic Revolution* published in Russian in August 1905 in Moscow, St. Petersburg and Geneva. In this book Lenin sets forth the theoretical basis of the decisions passed by the Third RSDLP Congress and of Bolshevik strategy and tactics in the bourgeois-democratic revolution. Basing himself on the founders of scientific communism Marx and Engels, Lenin further elaborates the thesis of the leading role of the proletariat in a bourgeois-democratic revolution, which, he maintains, must inevitably develop into a socialist revolution. Subsequent events were to prove correct the decisions taken at the Congress.

The photographs and documents in the next section of the display relate to the revolutionary struggle that was to develop throughout Russia in the spring and summer of 1905, with massive strikes in major industrial cities, unrest among the peasants

The battleship *Potemkin*. Model.

N. Lenin. Deux tactiques.
Prix. 1 fr. 25 cts. — 1 mk. — 18 ch. — 25 cent.
Россійская Соціальдемократическая Рабочая Партія.

Пролетаріи всѣхъ странъ соединяйтесь!

Н. ЛЕНИНЪ.

Двѣ тактики
СОЦІАЛЬДЕМОКРАТІИ
въ демократической
революціи.

Изданіе Центр. Ком. Р. С. Д. Р. П.

ЖЕНЕВА
Типографія Партіи. 3 rue de la Colline 3
1905

Cover of *Two Tactics of Social-Democracy in the Democratic Revolution*. 1905 edition.

and the first barricades blocking city streets. The Army and Navy joined the revolutionary movement. There is a photograph of the battleship *Potemkin* whose sailors were the first in the Black Sea Fleet to mutiny against the Tsar. A scale model of the battleship stands in the middle of the room. Later, Lenin would write that the mutiny on the *Potemkin* marked the first occasion on which a large unit of the armed forces openly sided with the revolution and that it was of immense importance as the first attempt to create the nucleus of a revolutionary army.

In October 1905 Russia was swept by a general political strike. The two million workers who took part demanded an end to the Tsarist regime and the proclamation of a democratic republic. For the first time in world history the striking workers set up their own mass organizations: the Councils, or Soviets of Workers' Deputies. The Soviets were highly valued by Lenin as leading bodies of the armed uprising and as embryos of people's power. One of the photographs is of a mass rally staged by striking textile workers in Ivanovo-Voznesensk. The rally elected a Council (Soviet) of Representatives which was to become a prototype of the Soviets of Workers' Deputies.

Early in November 1905 Lenin returned to Petersburg where he took charge of the Central and Petersburg Bolshevik Committees, addressed Party meetings and conferences, met Party activists, contributed to Bolshevik publications and took part in the preparations for an armed uprising.

On display is a copy of the Bolsheviks' first legal newspaper, *Novaya Zhizn* (The New Life). As chief editor Lenin approached the outstanding journalists, writers and dedicated Bolsheviks–M. Olminsky, V. Vorovsky, A. Lunacharsky and M. Gorky–with the request that they write for the paper. Contributions were also received from leading West-European revolutionaries such as Rosa Luxemburg, Karl Liebknecht, Marcel Cachin, Paul Lafargue, and others.

A talented journalist and editor Lenin understood his reader. His writing was always precise and he had a brilliant grasp of how best to make a point. Thirteen of his articles were published in *Novaya zhizn*. The issue on view contains a key work–"Party Organisation and Party Literature"–in which Lenin substantiates his principle of party commitment in literature. This principle, he insists, should become part and parcel of the common proletarian cause and serve millions of working people.

A show-case in the middle of the room contains copies of newspapers printed by the Bolsheviks in the towns of Central Russia and the outlying provinces. By the wall nearby is a scale model of an illegal printing press set up at a fruitseller's in Lesnaya Street in Moscow.

The Revolution culminated in an armed uprising in Moscow in December 1905. For nine days several thousand workers put up a heroic struggle against a superior force of police and government troops. The insurgents were supported by workers in many other industrial centres. A map shows the location of the fighting round the barricades in Moscow and other cities. Visitors can also see a slides show on the Moscow uprising.

Though the uprising was crushed, it had a tremendous impact. Lenin noted that the "unmatched heroism of the Moscow workers provided the toiling masses of Russia with a model in the struggle" to emulate.

After the defeat of the uprising the country was still in the grip of political strikes, peasant unrest and revolts and mutinies in the Army and Navy. Against this background and under the guidance of Lenin the RSDLP held its Fourth (Unity) and Fifth Congresses. During the heated debate with the Menshevik opposition the Party worked out specific methods enabling the masses to continue their struggle in the altered circumstances. In the stands relating to this period there are photographs of the People's House in Stockholm where the Fourth Congress was held in April 1906 and of a Reformed church building in suburban London where delegates gathered for the Fifth Congress in May 1907.

Lenin had to lead the Party and the revolutionary struggle of the working class in difficult conditions. Hunted by the police who had orders to arrest him at any cost he went into hiding. Late in the summer of 1906 he moved to Vaza cottage, Kuokkala, Finland. The cottage, which was rented by a comrade, stood by itself on the edge of a wood, which made it very suitable for underground activities. Lenin lived here on and off until December 1907. From Kuokkala he sometimes went secretly to Petersburg. In August 1907 he attended the Seventh Congress of the Second International in Stuttgart as one of the RSDLP delegates sent by the Party's Central Committee. Included among the exhibits is a photograph of the Congress meeting in Stuttgart.

The last section of the exhibition is devoted to the significance and influence of the 1905 Russian Revolution throughout the world. It had a considerable impact on the growth in revolutionary activities of workers and peasants in many countries and led to an upsurge in the national liberation movement in the colonial countries in the East. A map to the right of the entrance shows countries in Europe, Asia and Latin America where revolutionary upsurge was triggered off by the 1905-1907 events in Russia. Of exceptional interest are the copies of contemporary Social-Democratic newspapers (mounted on a revolving stand near the map)—*L'Humanité* (France), *Népszava* (Hungary) and *Rabotnicheski vestnik* (Bulgaria)—which have high praise for the valiant Russian workers.

"Without the 'dress rehearsal' of 1905, the victory of the October Revolution in 1917 would have been impossible," Lenin wrote.

EFFORTS TO STRENGTHEN THE PARTY IN THE YEARS OF THE REACTIONARY BACKLASH. LENIN'S DEFENCE AND FURTHER DEVELOPMENT OF MARXISM (1907-1910)

After it had suppressed the Revolution, the Tsarist government lashed out at the working-class movement and the Party. The photographs left of the entrance are of Felix Dzerzhinsky, Yakov Sverdlov, Grigory Ordjonikidze, Sergei Kirov, Mikhail Kalinin, Mikhail Frunze and others who were jailed or deported at that time. In accordance with a decision taken by the Bolshevik centre, Lenin secretly left Russia for Stockholm. He had to board ship from an island in the Gulf of Finland. It was December, and in order to reach the island he had to walk across thin ice. At a certain point, the ice began to crack: it was by a hair's breadth that Lenin escaped drowning. The crossing is the subject of a painting by A. Rylov hung in this room.

Awaiting Krupskaya's arrival in Stockholm, Lenin toured the sights of the city, and at the Royal

The house in Rue Marie-Rose in Paris where Lenin and Krupskaya lived from 1909 to 1912.

Library read and made notes on books banned in Russia. Joined by his wife, Lenin set off with her to Geneva where he resumed the publication of the *Proletary* (The Proletarian), a leading Bolshevik newspaper. The first few stands in the room display the articles he contributed to the *Proletary* including "Revolution and Counter-Revolution", "The Third Duma", "On the Assessment of the Russian Revolution" and others written to sum up the experience of the Revolution of 1905-1907 and to outline prospects for the revolutionary struggles. At that time Lenin went deeply into the agrarian question which determined the historical and national characteristics of the revolution in a country like Russia in which the peasant population predominated. On show are Lenin's manuscript of "The Agrarian Question in Russia at the End of the 19th Century" and an abstract he made of his book *The Agrarian Programme of the Social-Democrats in the First Russian Revolution of 1905-1907*. He prepared this abstract in the summer of 1908 at the request of the Polish Social-Democrats. It was published in their journal, *Przegląd Socjaldemokratyczny* in Polish. The book itself, which was printed in Petersburg in 1908, never reached the reader because it was destroyed on the instructions of the tsarist censors.

In the years of the post-Revolutionary reaction Lenin worked hard to preserve the Party and build up its links with the Russian working class. Among the exhibits in the room are photographs and documents relating to the Fifth All-Russia RSDLP Conference held in Paris late in December 1908. In its resolutions, the Conference stressed the importance of effectively combining illegal and legal methods of work. It condemned the opportunist tactics of the Mensheviks who had rejected the revolutionary programme of the Second Congress. These Mensheviks became known as the "Liquidators" because they sought dissolution (liquidation) of the underground party cells and the discontinuation of all underground activities.

On view is a photograph of the house where the Conference delegates convened and another of 4 Rue Marie-Rose where Lenin and his wife rented a flat between July 1909 and June 1912. They moved here after the *Proletary*'s editorial office had been shifted from Geneva to Paris. The flat became the centre for all sorts of meetings and debates. Lenin often put up his comrades, underground Party workers, who had secretly fled from Russia. Today, the house has been turned into a

Sculptural portrait of Lenin by Aronson.

museum by the French Communists.

In Paris Lenin studied the French working-class movement. He visited Paul Lafargue and his wife Laura, daughter of Karl Marx, in Draveilles, twenty kilometres from Paris. A watercolour of the Lafargues' house by Frédérick Longuet can be seen among a row of photographs at the end of the display. While living in Paris, Lenin gave lectures and made speeches both in the capital and in other French cities. He spoke on the Paris Commune and the situation in Russia and in the Party. Posters announcing his public appearances are on display. A photograph shows Lenin visiting Maxim Gorky in April 1908 on the Mediterranean island of Capri where the ailing writer was staying. Lenin made friends with Capri fishermen with whom he often went fishing.

In those years Lenin worked hard to counter the spread of reactionary ideology and to cut the ground from under the attempts to revise the philosophical foundations of Marxism. In May 1909 he published his book, *Materialism and Empirio-Criticism. Critical Comments on a Reactionary Philosophy* under the pen-name of Vl. Ilyin. While writing it he read hundreds of books on philosophy and the natural sciences, especially physics, in German, French and English. A copy of the first edition of *Materialism and Empirio-Criticism* is on view in the centre of the wall opposite the entrance. Some of the source books he studied are exhibited in display cases.

In *Materialism and Empirio-Criticism*, Lenin analyses the non-Marxist, idealistic philosophy. He exposes the latest techniques used by the exponents of idealism to defend their doctrine and then sets forth and further develops the key points in Marxist philosophy. His arguments are still successfully used by Communist parties to oppose modern non-Communist philosophies, philosophical revisionism and dogmatic interpretations of Marxism.

In special albums to the left and right of the first edition there are photocopies of separate pages of Lenin's book. Some of the books he read for, and quoted in *Materialism and Empirio-Criticism* are displayed on shelves on another wall. Also in this part of the room are photographs of the libraries in Paris and Geneva and a scale model of the British Museum's reading room where Lenin worked on *Materialism and Empirio-Criticism*. There are photographs of Lenin's elder sister Anna and the Bolsheviks M. T. Yelizarov and I. I. Skvortsov-Stepanov who helped with the publication of the book.

The last section in the room is devoted to materials relating to a meeting held under Lenin's chairmanship, in Paris in the summer of 1909 of the enlarged editorial board of the *Proletary* newspaper. The delegates spoke out against the anti-Party sentiment among some Party members depressed by the political reaction in Russia. These members became known as Otzovists because they demanded that the Party recall *(otozvat)* its deputies from the State Duma (Parliament). They also sought to draw the Party away from working within legal working-class organizations. The *Proletary* meeting stressed that the Bolshevik Party had nothing in common with the Otzovists, and they urged Party members to wage on unremitting struggle against them. Lenin's manuscripts in this section expose the treacherous stand taken by Trotsky who sought to unite the revolutionaries and the opportunists within a single party and spread Centrist ideas and tolerant attitudes to the opportunists within the Party.

The items in the last stand in the room relate to Lenin's work on uniting the Left-wing forces in the international working-class movement, and to his participation in the International Socialist Bureau of the Second International* and its Congresses. In a photograph in the top row of materials on display is a view of Copenhagen where Lenin attended the Eighth Congress of the Second International, and worked at the Royal Library, mostly reading books on Denmark's agriculture. The photograph placed next is a view of Stockholm where Lenin reported on the Copenhagen Congress at meetings of a group assisting the RSDLP. It was also in Stockholm in August and September 1910 that Lenin saw, for the last time, his mother Maria Alexandrovna who had come specially from Russia to meet her son. She died in St. Petersburg in July 1916.

Room No. 6

A NEW UPSURGE IN THE REVOLUTIONARY MOVEMENT (1910-1914)

The first section in the room is devoted to the main features of Russia's economic and political development in 1910-1914. In a stand to the left is a copy of Lenin's article "The Beginning of Demonstrations", in which he wrote, "The phase of the *total* domination of the Black-Hundred reaction has come to an end. The phase of a new upsurge is beginning. ... In the first Russian Revolution the proletariat taught the masses to fight for freedom, in the second revolution it must lead them to victory!"

The new upsurge in the revolutionary movement occurred in a changed economic situation. A diagram "The Main Indices of an Industrial Boom in Russia" shows that a period of depression was succeeded by a recovery in the main industries.

The conditions prevailing in Russia in 1910-1914 turned the working class into a decisive force in the fight against Tsarism and capitalism. The diagram, "The Strike Movement in Russia in 1910-1914" shows that whereas in 1910 there were only 222 strikes, eight of them political, in 1914 there were 3,534, 2,401 of them political.

Apart from encouraging the workers in their fight against the exploiters, the economic and political strikes also roused the peasantry to action. Lenin carefully analysed the situation in which the peasants found themselves after the so-called Stolypin agrarian reform which in effect did nothing to change the appalling conditions in which an overwhelming majority of them lived. In his articles, "The Last Valve", "Big Landlord and Small Peasant Landownership in Russia", and "What Is Happening in the Countryside?" (copies of which are on display) Lenin analyses the peasants' situation following the reform.

With the rise in the revolutionary movement, a working-class party could play a decisive role. However, the RSDLP was bitterly divided between the Bolsheviks on the one hand, and the Liquidators, the Conciliators and Trotsky, on the other.

Lenin exposes the divisive activities launched by the anti-Party groups and trends and lays bare the sources of Trotskyism in his articles, "The Historical Meaning of the Inner-Party Struggle in Russia", "The New Faction of Conciliators, or the Virtuous", and "Judas Trotsky's Blush of Shame" (copies are on display).

Forming part of the exhibition is an original copy of the first issue (December 16, 1910) of the *Zvezda* (The Star) newspaper containing Lenin's article, "Differences in the European Labour Movement" in which he describes the main deviations both in practice and theory from Marxism. Among the deviationists, he lists the revisionists, the opportunists and the reformists on the one hand, and anarchists, and anarcho-syndicalists on the other. He shows that these deviations were rooted in the structure of capitalist society and in the development of the class struggle.

There are also photostat copies of newspapers published abroad, and in Petersburg and Moscow in 1908-1912. These publications—*Rabochaya gazeta* (The Workers' Gazette), *Sotsial-Democrat*, *Zvezda*, and *Nevskaya zvezda* (The Neva Star), and the journals, *Mysl* (The Thought) and *Prosveshcheniye* (The Enlightenment)—carried Lenin's articles in which he urges all true Party supporters to strengthen their unity in order to protect Marxism, to combat the Liquidators and the Otzovists and to put an end to the crisis in the Party.

Above the first stand left of the entrance hangs a photograph of a house in the Paris suburb of Longjumeau. A Party school set up in the house on Lenin's initiative in the spring of 1911 trained revolutionary workers to become professional Party leaders. It also played a tremendous role in consolidating Party organizations on the Bolshevist principles. Lenin read most of the lectures.

To commemorate Lenin's stay in Longjumeau, the French Communists have put up a plaque on the wall of No. 91 (at the corner of La Rue de l'Ecole and La Grand Rue), which is inscribed as fol-

Lenin. 1910.

lows: "In 1911 V.I. Lenin, theoretician and leader of the world Communist movement and founder of the Soviet Union lived and worked here."

The display in Room 6 is centred round materials relating to the Fourth (Prague) All-Russia RSDLP Conference. On the upper part of the central wall is a big photograph of Prague. There is another photograph (in a stand) of the People's House in Hybernská Street in which the conference delegates met on January 5-17, 1912. There is also a scale model of the room where the delegates held their meetings.

At Lenin's suggestion the Conference declared itself a supreme Party body having the right to set up leading centres invested with full powers. As such, its task was to restore the local Party organizations. Lenin addressed the delegates with a report, "The Tasks of the Party in the Present Situation". The Conference passed a resolution (on display) which called on all revolutionary forces to rally under the Bolshevik banner.

The Conference expelled the Menshevik Liquidators from the Party, thus putting an end to the formal alliance with the Mensheviks. In February 1912, after the Conference Lenin wrote to Maxim Gorky, "We have finally succeeded–in spite of the liquidationist scoundrels–in reviving the Party and its Central Committee. I hope you will be as glad of this as we are."

The delegates passed a number of resolutions on international and national liberation movements and elected the Party's Central Committee. Photographs of Central Committee members–V. I. Lenin, F. I. Goloshchokin, G. K. Ordjonikidze, S. S. Spandaryan and others–are on view in a stand.

In June 1912 Lenin, Krupskaya and her mother moved from Paris to Cracow, which was then part of Austria-Hungary.* In a letter (displayed in a special stand) Lenin explains to Gorky the reasons for this decision, "You ask why I am in Austria. The C.C. has organized a Bureau here (between ourselves): the frontier is close by, we make use of it, it's nearer to Petersburg, we get the papers here on the third day, it's become far easier to write to the papers there, co-operation with them goes better."

Workers Reading Pravda. Sculptors R. Taurit, V. Isayeva, 1940.

Entrance to the house in Longjumeau, France, where there was a Party school directed by Lenin.

In the two years that Lenin stayed in Cracow the city became the Bolsheviks' ideological and organizational centre. The Central Committee did most of its work in Cracow which was visited by Party activists, and directives were sent from there to Party organizations in Russia.

There are photographs of the house where Lenin and his family lived in 1912-1914: 218 Zwierzyniec (now Królowej Jadwigi) Street, 47 Lubomirskiego (now Andrzeja Modrzewskiego) Street, and the house in Biały Dunajec near Poronin where Lenin stayed in the summer of 1913 and in 1914. To commemorate Lenin's stay in Poland, museums have been set up in Cracow and Poronin, and memorial plaques put on the houses in which he lived and worked.

In the situation of a revolutionary upswing, the Bolshevik newspapers began to play a more significant role. On April 22, 1912 the first issue of *Pravda* (Truth) came out. Lenin was heart and soul of the newspaper, its ideological leader and its editor-in-chief. Original copies of the newspaper are displayed on a central stand. *Pravda* printed more than 280 of his articles and other contributions. It was produced with money from workers whose love and trust it had aroused. The paper was closed down eight times, and every time it resumed publication under different names, such as *Rabochaya pravda, Severnaya pravda,* and *Za pravdu*. Original copies of the newspaper are on display together with photographs of *Pravda*'s editors and other members of its staff. The sculpture *Workers Reading "Pravda"* is by R. Taurit and V. Isayeva.

The exhibition continues with items on Lenin's guidance of the Bolshevik deputies in the Fourth State Duma* (Parliament). He constantly directed their activities, kept up a regular correspondence with them, met them, advised them and sketched outlines of their speeches.

On view is the original of "The RSDLP Election Platform" written by Lenin and other manuscripts of his works: "Concerning Certain Speeches by the Workers' Deputies", "The Question of the (General) Agrarian Policy of the Present Government", and "On the Question of National Policy". There are also a number of photographs of Bolshevik deputies who carried out important propaganda and organizational work among the masses.

A. Moravov's painting, *The Lena Massacre*, hangs in this room. On April 4, 1912 government soldiers opened fire at unarmed workers who were on strike at the Lena Goldfields in Siberia demanding higher pay and better working conditions. The shootings gave a powerful impetus to the revolutionary movement in Russia. The Bolshevik press spread the news of the tragic events throughout the country. In his article, "The Revolutionary Upswing", published in the *Sotsial-Demokrat* newspaper, Lenin wrote: "The Lena shootings led to the revolutionary temper of the masses developing into a revolutionary upswing of the masses."

In December 1912 and in the autumn of 1913, on Lenin's initiative, the Central Committee held a series of meetings attended by Party activists in order to decide on the next set of tasks to be tackled by the Party. The meetings strengthened the Party and consolidated its unity. In the "Notice" released by the RSDLP Central Committee to announce the meeting in Cracow, Lenin described 1912 as marking a historical turning point in the working-class movement in Russia. It was a year when the Bolshevik Party became stronger and increased its influence. In that year Russia had more strikes than any other advanced country; it had entered the climactic period of the new revolution.

The Cracow meeting concentrated on efforts to build up the Party and achieve greater unity in the working-class movement. "The unity of all trends and shades in the illegal organisation is absolutely necessary. Appeal for such unity," Lenin wrote in his theses "On the Attitude to Liquidationism and on Unity" (manuscript on display).

The Cracow meeting gave Party organizations specific instructions on how to guide the working-class movement in conditions of an impending, new revolution.

In the spring of 1913 Krupskaya's health took a turn for the worse and in May she and Lenin took a holiday in the village of Bialy Dunajec, near the Polish town of Poronin. Here, in the summer of 1913 and 1914 they stayed in the house of a peasant woman, Teresa Skupień. On view is an enlarged photo of Lenin taking a walk in the vicinity of Zakopane in the summer of 1914.

The holiday in Bialy Dunajec did not improve Lenin's wife's health and, in June 1913, they went to Berne, Switzerland, to consult a specialist. In August they returned to Poronin where in the autumn of 1913 the Central Committee had a conference with Party activists. The conference passed a number of documents drawn up by Lenin: "Resolution on the Organisational Question and on the Party Congress", "The Tasks of Agitation in the Present Situation", and "On the Party Press".

The other items shown here illustrate Lenin's work in further developing Party theory and its programme on the national question. By that time this matter had become particularly urgent, since the capitalists and landowners were intent on stirring up national strife so as to split the working class. This created a threat to the international working-class unity which the Bolsheviks had always worked for.

A resolution (a copy of which is on view) passed at the Poronin meeting on the national question says that the "interests of the working class demand the amalgamation of the workers of all nationalities of a given state in united proletarian organisations—political, trade union, co-operative, educational, etc." Other exhibits in this section include Lenin's articles "Critical Remarks on the National Question", "The Right of Nations to Self-Determination" and a number of other works in which he elaborates on the Marxist programme on the national question. Explaining the Party's policy on nationalities, Lenin treats the nationality question as part of the whole problem of the revolution, as a problem of the proletarians' allies in the fight for democracy, dictatorship of the proletariat and socialism.

In "Critical Remarks on the National Question" (1913) Lenin concludes that historically there were two tendencies in the national question under capitalism. One dominated at the time when capitalism was still in the making. This trend manifested itself in the awakening of national life and national movements, in opposition to any national oppression and in the establishment of one-nation states. The other tendency is characteristic of monopoly capitalism. It is marked by the development of relations between nations, the forcible breaking down of barriers between nations, and the establishment of international unity in the economy, politics, science, etc.

The Bolshevik programme on the national question took account of both trends. On the one hand it proclaimed the complete equality of nations and languages, maintained that no one nation should be given privileges at the expense of another, and insisted on a nation's right to self-determination including the right to secede and to independent statehood. On the other hand it proclaimed the principle of internationalism and declared war on bourgeois nationalism.

Another exhibit is a wooden scale model of the house in Poronin where the RSDLP Central Committee held its conference in September 1913.

The relief map at the end of the display shows the location of the Party organizations and illustrates the working-class movement in the years of the revolutionary upheaval of 1910-July 1914. As the revolutionary movement grew, more than a million and a half workers went on strike in the first six months of 1914, with disputes over pay and working conditions interspersed with political walkouts. The country was advancing towards a new revolution. The Bolsheviks were making preparations for another Congress but their plans were foiled by the outbreak of World War I in the summer of 1914. All their previous revolutionary activities had prepared the Bolsheviks led by Lenin to withstand the severe trials of the world war.

THE PARTY IN WORLD WAR I AND THE FEBRUARY REVOLUTION OF 1917 (1914-FEBRUARY 1917)

When the war broke out Lenin was in Poronin. He was arrested on a false denunciation by the Austrian authorities and imprisoned in the town of Nowy Targ. The stand to the left of the entrance displays M. Sokolov's watercolour, depicting Krupskaya visiting Lenin in prison, as well as a photograph of the prison cell in which Lenin spent eleven days. After his release Lenin left for Berne. On view in this room are a number of articles he wrote at the time including "The Tasks of Revolutionary Social-Democracy in the European War", "The Position and Tasks of the Socialist International", and "On the National Pride of the Great Russians". These articles reveal the attitude adopted by Lenin and the Bolsheviks towards an imperialist war. Lenin denounced World War I for its plunderous nature, defined its causes and formulated the tasks the war set before the Social-Democrats.

Lenin. 1914.

A picture in the room shows a summer cottage in Ozerki near Petrograd[1] where the Party held an All-Russia conference in November 1914 to discuss Lenin's articles on Bolshevik tactics in a war situation. A special display is devoted to "The War and Russian Social-Democracy", a manifesto issued by the RSDLP Central Committee. The Bolsheviks condemned the war as imperialist, predatory and unjust. Lenin insisted that the imperialist conflict should be turned into a civil war. In effect, this was a call for a revolution. In the manifesto Lenin urges the Social-Democrats to work for the defeat of "their own", i. e. Tsarist government in the imperialist war: "From the standpoint of the working class and of the toiling masses of all the nations of Russia, the defeat of the tsarist monarchy ... would be the lesser evil." This, he writes, would undoubtedly make it easier for the people to overthrow Tsarism. The tactics of defeating one's own government in a predatory war were aimed at turning it into a war waged by the oppressed against the oppressors and would lead eventually to the victory of the revolution. In the manifesto Lenin calls on the revolutionary Marxist parties to set up a Third International free of opportunists to replace the Second International which was a failure.

The Bolshevik deputies in the State Duma actively opposed the war describing it as imperialist. In November 1914 they were arrested and in February 1915 put on trial. A photograph above one of the stands shows the Bolshevik deputies of the Fourth State Duma G. I. Petrovsky, F. N. Samoilov, M. K. Muranov, A. Ye. Badayev, and N. R. Shagov. Also on view is an article, "What Has Been Revealed by the Trial of the Russian Social-Democratic Labour Duma Group", in which Lenin shows that thanks to the trial the Bolshevik political slogans had reached the broadest sections of the population.

The war was a severe test for political parties, a test of their loyalty to the interests of the working class and the cause of the socialist revolution.

Mounted on the central wall are manuscripts of Lenin's works, "Opportunism and the Collapse of the Second International", "Kautsky, Axelrod and Martov—True Internationalists", "What Next?", and "Under the False Flag" in which he exposes international opportunism, social-chauvinism and Centrism. He condemns the opportunists' treacherous actions and the shameful deals they had contracted with the bourgeoisie. In his articles of those years Lenin notes that as an international association of socialist parties the Second International had virtually ceased to exist with the start of the war: it had disintegrated into isolated social-chauvinist organizations which joined forces with their national bourgeoisie. He points out that as an organized tool operating on behalf of the bourgeoisie within the working-

[1] In August 1914 St. Petersburg was re-named Petrograd.

class movement, opportunism had turned into the proletariat's principal enemy. In "What Next?" (on display) he writes that the opportunists were bourgeois enemies of a proletarian revolution who secretly pursued their activities inside the workers' parties in peacetime and who became undisguised allies to the entire bourgeoisie at a time of crisis. From this he concludes that "the proletariat's unity in the struggle for the socialist revolution is its greatest weapon ."

In "An Appeal on the War" and "Socialism and War" (exhibited here) he reveals the essence and aims of the world war. He develops the Marxist doctrine on wars and on the socialists' attitude to wars, stressing that there was an inevitable link between war and the class struggle of the proletariat. In formulating their stand as regards war from a class point of view the Marxists-Leninists recognize the justice and the progressive character of revolutionary, national liberation wars fought to overthrow the bourgeoisie and for the victory of the socialist revolution. The message of the collection in the room can best be summed up in the following quotation from Marx which is prominently displayed: "An alliance between the workers of the world will finally root out all war."

On the wall left of the entrance is a photograph of a group of delegates who attended a conference of the RSDLP's foreign sections in Berne in February 1915. Displayed next to it are the agenda and materials of the conference published in a copy of the *Sotsial-Demokrat* newspaper dated March 29, 1915. The Berne conference, which was important for the entire Party, produced a platform uniting all the revolutionary internationalists in the world working-class movement. It also decided on specific measures to be taken in order to turn the imperialist war into a civil war.

In defining the policy of a Marxist party towards war, the Bolsheviks went beyond mere declarations of their intent. They launched into active underground secret revolutionary work among workers, soldiers, and sailors. In a letter (on display), Lenin wrote to A. G. Shlyapnikov, a Central Committee representative with special powers of authority, that "the Party's work has become a hundredfold more difficult, and yet we shall do it! *Pravda* has educated thousands of conscientious workers out of whom, in spite of all difficulties, another team of leaders will be formed as a Russian Central Committee for the party."

On view in the same section of the room is an article, "Several Theses" in which Lenin provides brief answers to key questions which had arisen in the revolutionary movement. He also outlines the tasks facing a proletarian party in Russia at war. Answering a question about what the Party would do were the revolution to put it in power in the present war, Lenin wrote, "... we would propose peace to *all* the belligerents on the condition that freedom is given to the colonies and *all* the peoples that are dependent, oppressed and deprived of rights." This is exactly how Lenin's Party saw its internationalist duty in the difficult conditions of war time. It showed all working-class parties how to fight for the interests of the working class, the working masses.

The exhibits in Room 7 illustrate how the Bolshevik Party, led by Lenin, worked for the unity of the workers of the world. An urgent task at the time was to set up a Third International. With this aim in mind, Lenin entered into a correspondence with Left-wing socialists in Bulgaria, Holland, Sweden, Norway and other countries. On view are photographs of prominent internationalist socialists and international working-class leaders.

Of great significance for the Bolsheviks' efforts to create the Third International were two international socialist conferences in Zimmerwald and in Kienthal in Switzerland. The village of Zimmerwald, a view of which can be seen in one of the stands, was the venue for the first international Socialist Conference on August 23-26, 1915. The Conference passed a manifesto (on view) urging a fight for peace. Although it suffered from inconsistencies and left out some vital points, Lenin signed it since it was "... a *step forward* towards a real struggle against opportunism, towards a rupture with it." The Conference showed that the ideas of the Russian revolutionary Marxists found ever increasing recognition among Western socialists.

The Left-wing revolutionary forces were united still closer by the second international Socialist Conference held in April 1916 in the village of Kienthal. The delegates focussed on the proposals of the Bolshevik Central Committee whose members directly linked the problems of peace with a socialist revolution.

Although it voted against the Bolshevik proposals for the imperialist war to be turned into a civil war, for the governments in each belligerent country to be defeated, and for a Third International to be set up, the Conference brought about greater unity among the internationalists on the ideological basis of Marxism-Leninism. It was another step towards rupture with the social-chauvinists.

Schweizerbund Café in Bern, Switzerland. A conference of the RSDLP section abroad was held there in February-March, 1915.

Н. ЛЕНИНЪ (ВЛ. ИЛЬИНЪ).

ИМПЕРІАЛИЗМЪ,

КАКЪ НОВѢЙШІЙ ЭТАПЪ

КАПИТАЛИЗМА.

(Популярный очеркъ).

СКЛАДЪ ИЗДАНІЯ:
Книжный складъ и магазинъ „Жизнь и Знаніе"
Петроградъ, Поварской пер., 2, кв. 9 и 10. Тел. 227—42.
1917 г.

Cover of *Imperialism, the Highest Stage of Capitalism*. The 1917 edition was entitled *Imperialism, the Latest Stage of Capitalism*.

On display are photographs of Berne and Zurich where Lenin and his wife spent three years. Life was hard as most of their earnings were royalties from Lenin's writings, and it was almost impossible to publish political, anti-war articles or books. He wrote, "Personally, I cannot earn much enough. Without that money I can just lie down and die. Things are hellishly expensive, and there is nothing to live on."

Lenin and his wife lived modestly and were content with simple furniture and clothes. Displayed in a stand are some objects that belonged to Lenin and his wife during their time as émigrés—an ink-well, a glass and glass-holder, a spoon for making tea and table knives.

Early in 1916 they moved from Berne to Zurich. There they stayed with the family of a shoemaker, Kammerer, until April 1917. It was quite an international household. The Kammerers, both Swiss, lived in two rooms; the occupants of a third room were the wife of a German soldier and her children, an Italian rented a fourth, and some Austrian actors a fifth room. The sixth room was let to the Russians, Lenin and Krupskaya. A memorial plaque which reads, "LENIN, leader of the Russian Revolution, lived here between February 21, 1916 and April 2, 1917" has been put up by the Zurich Municipal Council on the façade of the house beneath the windows of the room occupied by Lenin and his wife.

Apart from being a leader of the revolutionary movement in those war years, Lenin also contributed to revolutionary theory. The stands in the left half of the room are dedicated to *Imperialism, the Highest Stage of Capitalism*, a theoretical book whose writing involved the study of a large amount of literature and statistics. On display are copies of books which Lenin read while writing the above work: he made notes from 148 books and 232 articles all told. His preparatory materials which were subsequently published under the title, *Notebooks on Imperialism*, amount to 800 pages of text and reveal Lenin's method of research and his approach to his subject.

He began work on *Imperialism* early in 1916. Among the items in these stands are the plan and rough copies of the book, and postcards Lenin sent to his sister Maria Ulyanova and to his publisher M. N. Pokrovsky. In the Preface to the Russian edition dated April 26, 1917 Lenin warned that *Imperialism* was written in an allegorical manner "... to which tsarism compelled all revolutionaries to have recourse whenever they took up the pen to write a 'legal' work."

In the Preface to the 1920 French and German editions, Lenin wrote, "Imperialism is the eve of the social revolution of the proletariat." The quotation has been chosen as the motto for this section of the room. Also on display are pages from Lenin's manuscript of *Imperialism*. The book analyses in great detail for the first time the economic essence of imperialism as the highest and last stage of capitalism. Lenin defines imperialism as monopoly capitalism: parasitic, rotting and dying. He describes the conditions for its collapse and speaks about the necessity for and the inevitability of the replacement of capitalism by socialism.

Exhibited in the right part of the room are various materials in which Lenin develops the doctrine of the socialist revolution, its content, motive forces and conditions and forms of its development. Among the items on display is "On the Slogan for a United States of Europe", an article written in August 1915. In it, proceeding from the law he discovered about the unequal economic and political development of capitalism at its imperialist stage, Lenin concludes that initially socialism could only triumph in a few or perhaps even only in one capitalist country. He further evolves this thesis in another article he wrote in the autumn of 1916, "The Military Programme of the Proletarian Revolution". Yet another article completed in the autumn of 1916, "A Caricature of Marxism and 'Imperialist Economism'" describes the many ways for transition to socialism. Lenin stresses that "all nations will arrive at socialism—this is inevitable, but all will do so in not exactly the same way, each will contribute something of its own to some form of democracy, to some variety of the dictatorship of the proletariat, to the varying rate of socialist transformations in the different aspects of social life".

In "The Collapse of the Second International" (May-June 1915), Lenin stresses that a revolution cannot be imported. It can only result from each country's internal development, being brought about by objective causes, such as extreme aggravation of social contradictions and crises, conditions which he describes as a revolutionary situation. However, he points out that for a revolutionary situation to develop into a revolution it is essential that the objective conditions combine with a subjective factor, i. e., the ability of the revolutionary class to take massive revolutionary actions.

He believes that a Marxist party's leadership in the revolutionary struggle of the working class is of crucial importance for the victory of a socialist revolution.

Displayed in the same section are two articles, "The 'Disarmament' Slogan" and "The Question of Peace", on war and peace in the future socialist society. Lenin wrote that a revolution has to be able to defend itself although "disarmament is the ideal of socialism", and "an end to wars, peace among nations, the cessation of pillaging and violence—is our (the Bolsheviks—*Tr.*) ideal".

Petrograd in the days of the February Revolution.

Between December 1915 and February 1916 Lenin wrote a set of theses under a common title, "The Socialist Revolution and the Right of Nations to Self-Determination" which is, in fact, the

Bolshevik declaration on colonies and colonial nations. This is an issue which forms part and parcel of the socialist revolution, its reserves and its allies. The declaration emphasizes the direct support to be given by the proletarian revolution to the peoples in the colonies and the oppressed nations in general in their anti-imperialist struggle. Lenin writes that "the right of nations to self-determination implies exclusively the right to independence in the political sense", and points out that "this demand, therefore, is not the equivalent of a demand for separation ... and the formation of small states. It implies only a consistent expression of struggle against all national oppression."

In his "Reply to P. Kievsky (Yu. Pyatakov)", in "A Caricature of Marxism and 'Imperialist Economism'", and in a letter to Inessa Armand*, dated December 12, 1916, Lenin demonstrates the need for the fight for democracy to be coupled with the fight for socialism.

Thus, in the years of World War I, Lenin armed the Party with a theory of socialist revolution which he regarded as a vital, many-sided process in the fight for the dictatorship of the proletariat, for democracy and socialism.

This theory was borne out by its subsequent practical application in a number of countries in Europe, Asia and Latin America. The revolutionary developments in these countries have confirmed the theory of socialist revolution and enriched the historical experience of the Soviet Communist Party. They have enriched this theory with practical experience of the transition to socialism. This experience is reflected in the documents approved by the Communist and Workers' parties at their international conferences and in works written by outstanding leaders and statesmen from various nations.

The photographs in the first section of the Room 8 reflect the disastrous situation in Russia at the end of 1916; villages in ruins, industry ground to a halt, famine, defeat after defeat at the front. Summing up the plight of his country, Lenin wrote, "Life teaches. Life is *advancing*, through the defeat of Russia, towards a revolution in Russia."

In "Several Theses" (a copy of which is on view), Lenin outlines the specific tasks which the Russian proletariat and the Bolshevik Party had to accomplish in the conditions of an impending revolution. He points out that the Party goals remained as before: the overthrow of the autocratic regime, the establishment of a democratic republic, confiscation of landed estates, and the introduction of an eight-hour working day. Only a revolutionary-democratic dictatorship of the proletariat and the peasantry can form the social content of the impending revolution in Russia, he writes.

Above the second stand on the left wall there is a photograph

Burning Tsarist emblems in Petrograd. February 1917.

of the People's House in Zurich. It was here that Lenin addressed young workers who had gathered on January 9, 1917 to mark the 12th anniversary of the First Russian Revolution. His words, "We must not be deceived by the present gravelike stillness in Europe. Europe is pregnant with revolution", proved prophetic. In slightly less than a month a bourgeois-democratic revolution broke out in Russia and overthrew the Tsarist regime in February 1917. The working class acted as leader and the chief motive force in the Revolution. The revolutionary workers and peasants were united under the guidance of the Bolshevik Party led by Lenin.

A painting, *It Has Come True at Last,* by S. Lukin (opposite the entrance) shows the throne room in the middle of which stands a soldier with a lowered rifle. The throne in the background is no longer a symbol of the Tsar's power, but merely an empty seat. Photographs to the right show Tsarist emblems being burnt near the Anichkov Bridge in Petrograd. Others are of rallies and demonstrations in various cities in Russia. Beneath the picture in a special display is the manifesto, "To All Citizens of Russia", issued by the Central Committee of the RSDLP on February 27, 1917. It reads in part as follows: "With a tremendous effort, shedding blood and losing lives, the Russian people have shaken off the slavery that has lasted for ages."

During the February Revolution Soviets of Workers' and Soldiers' Deputies were set up—organs of the revolutionary democratic dictatorship of workers and peasants. However, the Mensheviks and the Socialist Revolutionaries who dominated in most of the Soviets betrayed the people's cause and handed over power to a bourgeois Provisional Government,*

Lenin among a group of Russian émigrés on their way to Russia. Stockholm, March 31, 1917.

which resulted in the establishment of dual power* in the country. The task now facing the Bolshevik Party was to get all power handed over to the Soviets.

The new goals confronting the proletariat and the Bolshevik Party are set forth in Lenin's "Draft Theses", "To Our Comrades in War-Prisoner Camps", "The Tasks of the Proletariat in Our Revolution" and in "Telegram to the Bolsheviks Leaving for Russia" exhibited in the room.

"Our next duty is to spread our efforts, to organize the masses and to awaken new strata (of the population) ... as part of the preparations for all power to be taken over by the *Soviets of the Workers' Deputies,*" Lenin wrote in a letter to A. M. Kollontai* on March 17, 1917.

Displayed in the room are five of Lenin's "Letters From Afar", a leaflet, "To Our Comrades in War-Prisoner Camps", and the "Farewell Letter to the Swiss Workers". In these writings Lenin reveals the essence of the February Revolution, describes its motive forces, and defines the tasks facing the proletariat and the Bolshevik Party who had opted for a transition from bourgeois-democratic revolution to socialist revolution.

Lenin longed to return to Russia. This was extremely difficult, as part of his route lay across Germany, a nation at war with Russia. After overcoming numerous obstacles, Lenin, Krupskaya and thirty other Russian émigrés, nineteen of them Bolsheviks, left Switzerland on March 27 and travelled to Russia via Germany, Sweden, and Finland. An enlarged photograph shows Lenin and his comrades in Stockholm on their way home. A glass case to the right of the entrance displays Lenin's personal belongings and his travelling-bag.

THE GUIDING SPIRIT OF THE REVOLUTION (MARCH-OCTOBER 1917)

Lenin arrived in Petrograd late on the evening of April 3, 1917. A map traces the route by which he returned to Russia. On view are the questionnaire he filled in before crossing the border post at Tornio (Finland) on April 2, and the telegram he sent to his sisters Maria Ulyanova and Anna Yelizarova-Ulyanova: "Arriving 11 pm Monday. Inform *Pravda*. Ulyanov."

At 23:10 the train pulled in at the Finland station. In the square outside a large crowd of Petrograd workers gathered to welcome their leader. Climbing on to an armoured car, Lenin made a speech which ended with the words, "Long live the socialist revolution!" This event forms the subject of a sculpture (1925) by M. Manizer in the middle of the room.

In an armoured car Lenin, surrounded by crowds of people, left for a city mansion which in 1917 was occupied by the Bolsheviks'

Central and Petrograd Committees, their Military Organization and by a number of other agencies. Several times that night he went out onto the balcony to address the workers, soldiers and sailors who had gathered in the street below. Early in the morning, accompanied by his wife, Nadezhda Krupskaya, he moved to the flat of his sister, Anna Yelizarova-Ulyanova and her husband Mark Yelizarov (Flat 24, 48/9 Ulitsa Shirokaya, now 52 Ulitsa Lenina).

Lenin stayed at his sister's from April 4 to July 5, 1917. All this time was taken up by massive propaganda work to organize and rally the revolutionary forces round the Soviets. He took charge of the Party's Central Committee and of *Pravda* newspaper. The "April Theses" which he first formulated in March 1917 and published in *Pravda* on April 7, 1917 as "The Tasks of the Proletariat in the Present Revolution" played a major role in preparing the masses for the socialist revolution. The first draft of the "April Theses" and a copy of the April 7 edition of *Pravda* are the subject of a special display on the wall left of the entrance.

The Theses contain a detailed and theoretically well-grounded plan for transition from a bourgeois-democratic revolution, which had given power to the bourgeoisie, to a socialist revolution which was to put in power the working class and the poorest peasants.

In this work, Lenin provides a theoretical basis for the concept of Republic of Soviets, as a political form of the dictatorship of the proletariat, as a new and superior form of democracy.

The attitude to war, the most topical issue of the day, is ex-

Lenin addressing the Seventh All-Russia RSDLP(B) Conference held at the Taurida Palace. April 1917. Petrograd.

amined in the Theses. In view of the essentially bourgeois nature, aims and politics of its Provisional Government, the war for Russia's part remained a war of plunder. Only a government which would put the country on the road to socialism could restore peace to the nation, provide food for the starving and people with freedom. This idea is reflected in the Bolshevik slogans which revoked support for the Provisional Government and called for all power to the Soviets.

The Theses formulated the economic platform for the proletarian party in the revolution. The key points in the platform were nationalisation of all land in the country, which entailed the expropriation of landed estates. Once private land tenure had been abolished all land was to be put at the disposal of the local Soviets of Agricultural Labourers' and Peasants' Deputies. All banks were to be amalgamated into one national bank and put under the control of the Soviets of Workers' Deputies. The workers were to control all industry and all distribution of goods.

On internal party matters Lenin proposed that a Congress be convened so as to change the Party's programme, to include as one of its aims the creation of a Soviet Republic, and to rename the RSDLP—the Russian Communist Party. All revolutionary Marxists, Lenin suggested, should take as their goal the establishment of a third Communist International.

One of the stands in the room is devoted to various documents of the Seventh (April) All-Russia Conference of the Bolshevik Party, the first legal gathering the Bolsheviks held in Russia. The work of the Conference was guided by Lenin who delivered reports on the current situation, the agrarian question and the revision of the Party's programme. The Conference in effect amounted to a full party congress; it elected a new Central Committee led by Lenin.

After the Conference the Bolsheviks' aim in their struggle for a socialist revolution was to unite into a single revolutionary stream the peace movement of all democratic elements, the peasants' fight for land, and the national liberation movement of oppressed peoples.

The Bolsheviks had to explain to the proletariat, to all working people, the essence of their programme and platform, expose the Provisional Government as an enemy of the people and the Mensheviks and Socialist Revolutionaries as adherents of a conciliatory policy.

The entire wall to the right of the entrance is taken up by I. Brodsky's painting, *Lenin Addresses Workers at the Putilov Works* in May 12 (25), 1917* (1929), which conveys the atmosphere of the time. The workers who attended the meeting say Lenin spoke so clearly and simply that the people listening to him cast aside all doubts and hesitations and were ready to overcome all obstacles.

A former Putilov worker, P. A. Danilov recalls, "What Lenin said carried us away and filled us with enthusiasm. Fear and fatigue vanished. It seemed as though it was not he alone who spoke, but all the forty thousand workers present–whether sitting, standing or balancing on something. He was uttering their most cherished dreams. It seemed that everything that was in the workers' minds and hearts was uttered by the single voice of Lenin. Our inner thoughts and feelings which we had not conveyed to our fellow-workers for lack of a suitable moment or the right words, had suddenly been given expression and were spoken aloud. This meeting was historically momentous. It moved the Putilov masses,

The shooting down of a peaceful march of workers and soldiers. July 4, 1917. Petrograd.

and they moved into the revolution."

One of the exhibits is a shorthand copy of a speech on the attitude to the Provisional Government given by Lenin at the First All-Russia Congress of the Soviets of Workers' and Soldiers' Deputies early in June 1917. After declaring that the Bolshevik Party was ready to assume all power, Lenin explained the Bolsheviks' main aims: All power to the Soviets, bread to the working people, land to the peasants, and peace to all peoples. A copy of *Pravda* for July 2, 1917 on display contains Lenin's second speech at the Congress dealing with war.

On one of the walls is a diagram "The Bolshevik press early in July 1917". At that time the Party had 55 or so newspapers and magazines with a daily circulation of over five hundred thousand copies. The most popular of these was *Pravda* which published Lenin's articles virtually every day. From the date of his arrival in Russia to July 1917 Lenin contributed nearly 170 items to *Pravda*.

Lenin in hiding at Razliv. Sculptor V. Pinchuk.

Some of the materials in the room relate to the massive workers' protest demonstrations against the continuation of the war and the policies of the bourgeois government. A dramatic photograph taken in July in Petrograd records the shooting of peaceful demonstrators—workers and soldiers. Workers were subjected to mass searches, revolutionary regiments were disarmed,

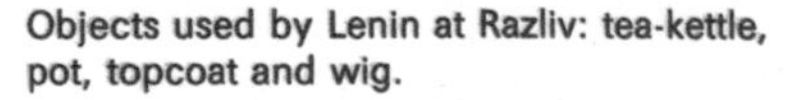

Objects used by Lenin at Razliv: tea-kettle, pot, topcoat and wig.

and their soldiers arrested. The Bolshevik Party and workers' organisations were the targets of severe reprisals.

In the morning of July 5, officer cadets* loyal to the Provisional Government ransacked *Pravda*'s offices and on July 7 the government issued a warrant to arrest Lenin and other prominent Bolsheviks and put them on trial. The Central Committee decided that Lenin should go into hiding in the suburbs of Petrograd. The settlement of Sestroretsk was chosen, most of whose inhabitants were workers from the local firearms factory. Lenin was put up by the Bolshevik worker N. A. Yemelyanov who lived not far from the Razliv railway station. There is a photograph, "The Shed with Hayloft Outside Yemelyanov's House at Razliv Station Where Lenin Went into Hiding in July 1917."

The situation following the July developments called for a revision of Party tactics and aims. On July 10 Lenin wrote "The Political Situation" (the manuscript is exhibited in a stand). "All hopes for a peaceful development of the Russian revolution have vanished for good," he wrote. Thus in the post-July period the problem of changing tactics and fighting methods became particularly pressing. The convening of another Party Congress was also a matter of great urgency.

The last display case in the room contains documents and materials of the Sixth Bolshevik Party Congress. It was held virtually illegally in a very complex situation late in July and early in August 1917, in Petrograd. Most of the delegates were revolutionaries, steeled in the struggle against the Russian autocracy and the bourgeoisie. On display there are materials relating to Lenin's election as delegate to the Congress by the Bolshevik Party organization in Yekaterinburg (now Sverdlovsk) in the Urals.

During preparations for the Congress and while it was in progress Lenin was in hiding from where he kept in close touch with the Party's Central Committee. His theses, "The Political Situation", pamphlet *On Slogans*, article "Lessons of the Revolution" and other works formed the basis for the Congress' decisions.

The Congress' resolution, "The Political Situation" (a copy of which is on display), sets the Party the following aim: to eliminate the counter-revolutionary bourgeois dictatorship and achieve a take-over of power by the working class and the poorest peasants via an armed uprising.

Other Congress resolutions on display in the room (to the right of the entrance) are: "The Economic Situation", "The Tasks of the Trade Union Movement", "The Youth Alliances", and "On Propaganda". There are also copies of the Party Rules with amendments approved by Congress delegates.

The Congress elected a new Central Committee led by Lenin. Hanging above the stand containing the Congress resolutions are photographs of Central Committee members who were active participants in the Revolution.

To be seen in the room is a manifesto issued by the Central Committee after the Congress urging the working class, soldiers and peasants to prepare for decisive battles with the bourgeoisie. "Our Party marches into battle with its banners unfurled," reads the manifesto.

The exhibits in Room 10 relate to Lenin's plan for an armed uprising and illustrate the victory of the 1917 October Revolution and its world-wide historical significance.

The first item on display is *The State and Revolution*, a work which Lenin finished writing in August-September 1917. It is a complete and systematic presentation of the Marxist view of the state. The book's theme is illustrated by its sub-title, "The Marxist Theory of the State and the Tasks of the Proletariat in the Revolution". In the situation of an impending socialist revolution in Russia and a number of other countries, the origins and role of the state and its future development acquired special theoretical and practical significance "as a practical question demanding immediate action, and, moreover, action on a mass scale" and as "the problem of explaining to the masses what they will have to do before long to free themselves from capitalist tyranny".

Also on view is the manuscript of the preparatory materials for *The State and Revolution*, the famous blue notebook otherwise known as *Marxism on the State*. The 48-page long manuscript is in Lenin's characteristic small handwriting. On the blue title cover is a list of works by Marx and Engels which Lenin studied when he was writing *Marxism on the State*. The manuscript which is of significance in its own right makes possible an acquaintance with Lenin's methods in working with source material.

In *The State and Revolution* pages of whose manuscript are displayed in several show-cases and stands, Lenin develops Marx's and Engels' views on the state. He stresses, "The state is a product and a manifestation of the *irreconcilability* of class antagonisms. The state arises where, when and insofar as class antagonisms objectively *cannot* be reconciled." He further points out that a victorious socialist revolution would result in the bourgeois state being replaced by the dictatorship of the proletariat, a state whose social foundation he viewed as a union between the working class and millions of toiling peasant masses.

He demonstrates that a Communist party had a decisive role to play not only in the establishment, but also in the consolidation of the dictatorship of the proletariat and in the building of socialism and communism. He also examines every aspect of proletarian democracy–a democracy of a superior type. He elaborates on the Marxist doctrine dealing with socialism and communism as two distinct phases of communist society and on the conditions in which the state withers away. The extensive dis-

Smolny Palace during the October armed uprising.

play dedicated to *The State and Revolution* includes the first Russian edition of the book and editions in various other languages.

As has already been mentioned the Central Committee hid Lenin from persecution by the Provisional Government in N. A. Yemelyanov's house near Razliv station, close to the Finnish border. However the situation in the area was almost as alarming as in the capital. Therefore Lenin was soon moved, disguised as a Finnish hay-maker, to a straw hut on the banks of Lake Sestroretsky Razliv. On view are items relating to this period in Lenin's life: photographs of his hideouts and some of the things he used when he lived in the straw hut. Lenin jokingly called the hut "my home", and the small patch cleared of bush outside it "my green study". He continued to work hard even though the conditions in which he lived and wrote were far from comfortable.

From his hideout Lenin maintained regular contact with the Central Committee through Grigori Ordjonikidze, A. V. Shotman, Eino Rahja and others. However, autumn soon came, and to go around dressed as a hay-maker could arouse suspicion. Besides, police sleuths with dogs had appeared in the vicinity of Sestroretsk. Lenin obviously had to be transferred to a safer place and the Central Committee decided to send him to Finland. Early in August Lenin travelled there, disguised as a stoker, on a train.

The coat and wig he wore on his way to Finland are on display. The photos in this section are of

A scale model of the cruiser *Aurora*.

Finnish Social Democrats A. Blomquist, Juho Latukka, Kustaa Rovio and Hugo Jalava who helped Lenin when he was in hiding in Finland. A map on the wall indicates the location of Lenin's last hideouts. A picture by D. Nalbandyan depicts him in hiding in Finland.

The next section of the display is devoted to the critical situation in Russia. As the war entered its fourth year the country's economic situation grew considerably worse. Railway transport was disrupted. Supplies of raw materials, coal and metal to industry were steadily diminishing. As production of coal, iron and steel and consumer goods dwindled, Russia was threatened with famine and mass unemployment. It was against this background that Lenin wrote *The Impending Catastrophe and How to Combat It*, a pamphlet in which he sets out a programme showing how to avoid and overcome catastrophe, and breathe new life into the country's economy. He also works out measures which could save Russia from ruin and starvation. These measures were as follows: nationalization of banks, insurance companies, and industries owned by monopolies; nationalization of land; abolition of commercial secrets; the compulsory merging of smaller capitalist-owned industries into major syndicates; and the institution of consumer societies. The purpose of this last measure was to make everyone bear an equal share of the burden of war and to have the poor classes control the consumption of the rich. "Control, supervision and accounting are the prime requisites for combatting the catastrophe and famine," Lenin concludes. He also suggests that an end be put to the war which, he points out, had accelerated the transition of monopoly capitalism to a state monopoly stage. This had brought mankind

Red Guard detachments. Petrograd.

even closer to socialism. "Perish or forge full steam ahead. That is the alternative put by history," he says. The manuscript of his pamphlet is on display.

In *Can the Bolsheviks Retain State Power?* (on view) Lenin emphasizes that Russia had both the economic and political prerequisites for a socialist revolution. He elaborates on the doctrine of the Soviets as a form of the dictatorship of the proletariat. Together with the pamphlet there is a facsimile copy of the following quote from Lenin: "It is only when the 'lower classes' *do not want to* live in the old way and the 'upper classes' *cannot carry on in the old way* that the revolution can triumph."

Photographs, documents and charts testify to the growing crisis in Russia: a massive working-class revolutionary movement, rising unrest among the peasants, a growth in the liberation movement of the oppressed inhabiting Russia nationalities, mounting revolutionary sentiment in the army. In this situation the Bolshevik Party's influence and authority among the masses greatly increased, as is shown in a chart, "The Alignment of Forces Between Political Parties on the Eve of the 1917 October Revolution". There were 350,000 members of the Party by the time the Revolution took place.

The Bolshevik Party possessed a clear-cut programme for the revolutionary transformation of society. It united into a single revolutionary force the workers' fight for socialism, the nationwide peace movement, the peasants' fight for land and the national liberation movement. It led the masses to victory in a socialist revolution.

Lenin's talent for a realistic assessment of a given situation and his political vision was fully revealed in the crisis. He focussed all his knowledge, his enormous political experience, will power and energy on preparations for an armed uprising. In "Marxism and Insurrection", "Advice of an Onlooker", "The Bolsheviks Must Assume Power" and other works (on display in the room) he sets forth his plan to organize an uprising which, against the background of the situation developing in Russia at the time, he describes as "a special type of political struggle".

In a stand to the left of the entrance is the manuscript of the article "The Crisis Has Matured", in which Lenin wrote, "The crisis has matured. The whole future of the Russian revolution is at stake."

In view of the growing revolutionary crisis in the country, Lenin asked the Central Committee to allow him to return to Petrograd. On display is an excerpt from the minutes of the RSDLP(B) Central Committee meeting held on October 3, 1917: "... to suggest to Ilyich (Lenin) that he come to Petrograd to make possible constant and close links." Early in October Lenin arrived secretly in the city where he stayed in M. V. Fofanova's flat (Flat 41, 1 Ulitsa Serdobolskaya). This was to be his last clandestine address in Petrograd.

Once in the capital, Lenin be-

№ 208.
Пятница,
27 октября 1917 г.

ЦѢНА:
въ Петроградѣ 15 коп.
на ст. жел. д. 18 коп.

ИЗВѢСТІЯ

Центральнаго Исполнительнаго Комитета и Петроградскаго Совѣта Рабочихъ и Солдатскихъ Депутатовъ.

Адресъ конторы: Лиговка, Сайкинъ пер., д. № 6. Телефонъ № 218-41.
Адресъ редакціи: Смольный Институтъ, 2-й этажъ комната № 144. Телефонъ № 38-89.

Декретъ о мирѣ,

принятый единогласно на засѣданіи Всероссійскаго Съѣзда Совѣтовъ Рабочихъ, Солдатскихъ и Крестьянскихъ Депутатовъ 26 октября 1917 г.

Рабочее и крестьянское правительство, созданное революціей 24—25 октября и опирающееся на Совѣты Рабочихъ, Солдатскихъ и Крестьянскихъ Депутатовъ предлагаетъ всѣмъ воюющимъ народамъ и ихъ правительствамъ начать немедленно переговоры о справедливомъ демократическомъ мирѣ.

Справедливымъ или демократическимъ миромъ котораго жаждетъ подавляющее большинство истощенныхъ, измученныхъ и истерзанныхъ войной рабочихъ и трудящихся классовъ всѣхъ воюющихъ странъ—миромъ, котораго самымъ опредѣленнымъ и настойчивымъ образомъ требовали русскіе рабочіе и крестьяне послѣ сверженія царской монархіи,—такимъ миромъ правительство считаетъ немедленный миръ безъ аннексій (т. е. безъ захвата чужихъ земель, безъ насильственнаго присоединенія чужихъ народностей) и безъ контрибуцій.

Такой миръ предлагаетъ Правительство Россіи заключить всѣмъ воюющимъ народамъ немедленно, выражая готовность сдѣлать безъ малѣйшей оттяжки тотчасъ-же всѣ рѣшительные шаги впредь до окончательнаго утвержденія всѣхъ условій такого мира полномочными собраніями народныхъ представителей всѣхъ странъ и всѣхъ націй.

Подъ аннексіей или захватомъ чужихъ земель Правительство понимаетъ сообразно правовому сознанію демократіи вообще, и трудящихся классовъ въ особенности всякое присоединеніе къ большому или сильному государству малой или слабой народности безъ точно, ясно и добровольно выраженнаго согласія и желанія этой народности, независимо отъ того, когда это насильственное присоединеніе совершено, независимо также отъ того насколько развитой или от сталой является насильственно присоединяемая или насильственно удерживаемая въ границахъ даннаго государства нація. Независимо, наконецъ, отъ того, въ Европѣ или въ далекихъ заокеанскихъ странахъ эта нація живетъ.

Если какая бы то ни была нація удерживается въ границахъ даннаго государства насиліемъ, если ей, вопреки выраженному съ ея стороны желанію—все равно, выражено ли это желаніе въ печати, въ народныхъ собраніяхъ, въ рѣшеніяхъ партій или возмущеніяхъ и возстаніяхъ противъ національнаго гнета—не представляется права свободнымъ голосованіемъ, при полномъ выводѣ войска присоединяющей или вообще болѣе сильной націи, рѣшить безъ малѣйшаго принужденія вопросъ о формахъ государственнаго существованія этой націи, то присоединеніе ея является аннексіей, т. е. захватомъ и насиліемъ.

Продолжать эту войну изъ-за того, какъ раздѣлить между сильными и богатыми націями захваченныя ими слабыя народности, Правительство считаетъ величайшимъ преступленіемъ противъ человѣчества и торжественно заявляетъ свою рѣшимость немедленно подписать условія мира, прекращающаго эту войну на указанныхъ равно справедливыхъ для всѣхъ безъ изъятія народностей условіяхъ.

Вмѣстѣ съ тѣмъ Правительство заявляетъ, что оно отнюдь не считаетъ вышеуказанныхъ условій мира ультимативными, т. е. соглашается разсмотрѣть и всякія другія условія мира, настаивая лишь на возможно болѣе быстромъ предложеніи ихъ какой бы то ни было воюющей страной и на полнѣйшей ясности, на безусловномъ исключеніи всякой двусмысленности и всякой тайны при предложеніи условій мира.

Тайную дипломатію Правительство отмѣняетъ, со своей стороны выражая твердое намѣреніе вести всѣ переговоры совершенно открыто передъ всѣмъ народомъ, приступая немедленно къ полному опубликованію тайныхъ договоровъ, подтвержденныхъ или заключенныхъ правительствомъ помѣщиковъ и капиталистовъ съ февраля по 25 октября 1917 года. Все содержаніе этихъ тайныхъ договоровъ, поскольку оно направлено, какъ это въ большинствѣ случаевъ бывало къ доставленію выгодъ и привилегій русскимъ помѣщикамъ и капиталистамъ, къ удержанію или увеличенію аннексій великороссовъ, Правительство объявляетъ безусловно и немедленно отмѣненнымъ.

Обращаясь съ предложеніемъ къ правительствамъ и народамъ всѣхъ странъ начать немедленно открытые переговоры о заключеніи мира, Правительство выражаетъ съ своей стороны готовность вести эти переговоры, какъ посредствомъ письменныхъ сношеній, по телеграфу, такъ и путемъ переговоровъ между представителями разныхъ странъ или на конференціи таковыхъ представителей. Для облегченія такихъ переговоровъ Правительство назначаетъ своего полномочнаго представителя въ нейтральныя страны.

Правительство предлагаетъ всѣмъ правительствамъ и народамъ всѣхъ воюющихъ странъ немедленно заключить перемиріе, причемъ со своей стороны, считаетъ желательнымъ, чтобы это перемиріе было заключено не меньше, какъ на три мѣсяца, т. е. на такой срокъ, въ теченіе котораго вполнѣ возможно, какъ завершеніе переговоровъ о мирѣ съ участіемъ представителей всѣхъ безъ изъятія народностей или націй, втянутыхъ въ войну или вынужденныхъ къ участію въ ней, такъ равно и созывъ полномочныхъ собраній народныхъ представителей всѣхъ странъ для окончательнаго утвержденія условій мира.

Обращаясь съ этимъ предложеніемъ мира къ правительствамъ и народамъ всѣхъ воюющихъ странъ, временное рабочее и крестьянское правительство Россіи обращается также въ особенности къ сознательнымъ рабочимъ трехъ самыхъ передовыхъ націй человѣчества и самыхъ крупныхъ участвующихъ въ настоящей войнѣ государствъ, Англіи, Франціи и Германіи. Рабочіе этихъ странъ оказали наибольшія услуги дѣлу прогресса и соціализма и великіе образцы чартистскаго движенія въ Англіи, рядъ революцій, имѣвшихъ всемірно-историческое значеніе, совершенныхъ французскимъ пролетаріатомъ, наконецъ, въ геройской борьбѣ противъ исключительнаго закона въ Германіи и образцовой для рабочихъ всего мира длительной, упорной дисциплинированной работѣ созданія массовыхъ пролетарскихъ организацій Германіи. Всѣ эти образцы пролетарскаго героизма и историческаго творчества служатъ намъ порукой за то, что рабочіе названныхъ странъ поймутъ лежащія на нихъ теперь задачи освобожденія человѣчества отъ ужасовъ войны и ея послѣдствій, что эти рабочіе всесторонней рѣшительной и беззавѣтно энергичной дѣятельностью своей помогутъ намъ успѣшно довести до конца дѣло мира и вмѣстѣ съ тѣмъ дѣло освобожденія трудящихся и эксплоатируемыхъ массъ населенія отъ всякаго рабства и всякой эксплоатаціи.

Decree on Peace adopted unanimously at the All-Russia Congress of Soviets of Workers', Soldiers' and Peasants' Deputies. October 26, 1917.

gan vigorous preparations for the armed uprising. On October 10 the Central Committee passed a resolution (on display) which stressed that an uprising was inevitable and timely, and that the Party's entire work should be subordinated to the organization and control of an armed uprising. The Committee set up a Politbureau headed by Lenin to ensure the political guidance of the uprising.

An enlarged meeting of the Central Committee on October 16 elected a Military-Revolutionary Committee. Preparations for the armed uprising began throughout the country.

On a stand is a letter which Lenin wrote on October 24 to the Central Committee members,

"I am writing these lines on the evening of the 24th. The situation is critical in the extreme. In fact it is now absolutely clear that to delay the uprising would be fatal.

"With all my might I urge comrades to realise that everything now hangs by a thread; that we are confronted by problems which are not to be solved by conferences or congresses (even congresses of the Soviets), but exclusively by peoples, by the masses, by the struggle of the armed people.

"...We must at all costs, this very evening, this very night, arrest the government, having first disarmed the officer cadets (defeating them, if they resist), and so on.

"... History will not forgive revolutionaries for procrastinating when they could be victorious today (and they certainly will be victorious today), while they risk losing much tomorrow, in fact, they risk losing everything."

Late on the night of October 24 Lenin went to the Smolny Institute*, the headquarters of the Revolution. At Smolny he assumed full leadership of the uprising. A scale model of Smolny is on view.

One section of the room is devoted to the armed uprising in Petrograd on October 24-25. A map with electric lights indicates the progress of the Revolution in the Russian capital, there is a photographic collage "The Bolsheviks: Active Participants in the 1917 October Revolution in Petrograd" and other photographs. One of these shows pickets of soldiers and sailors checking the papers of those who enter the Smolny Institute, the headquarters of the uprising. Commanders of revolutionary regiments and representatives from factories converged on Smolny from all over the city to get their instructions. Outside the building there were noisy crowds of sailors, soldiers and workers. Cars, lorries and armoured vehicles rumbled to and fro, as artillery pieces and machine-guns were put into position and firewood stacked together in case it proved necessary to erect barricades. At night bonfires lit up the square.

By the morning of October 25 all the strategic positions in the city—bridges across the Neva, the central telephone exchange, the telegraph, the power stations, and the railway stations were in the hands of the forces of the revolution. The Military-Revolution-

Lenin. January 1918.

ary Committee issued an appeal written by Lenin "To the Citizens of Russia" announcing that the bourgeois Provisional Government had been deposed and that all power had passed into the hands of the Soviets. Lenin's manuscript of the manifesto and a leaflet giving its text are on view.

Addressing an emergency meeting of the Petrograd Soviet at 2.35 p.m. on October 25 Lenin said, "the workers' and peasants' revolution, about the necessity of which the Bolsheviks have always spoken, has been accomplished".

In the evening the guns of the cruiser *Aurora* sounded the signal for the storming of the Winter Palace where the Provisional Government had taken refuge. Within the space of a few hours' the revolutionary forces had taken the palace.

Total victory had been won by the revolutionary workers, soldiers and sailors. A scale model of the *Aurora* is to be seen in the room.

At 4 a.m. on October 26 the Second All-Russia Congress of Soviets issued an appeal, "To Workers, Soldiers and Peasants", written by Lenin. The appeal (a copy is on view) proclaimed that state power, both in the capital and provinces, had passed into the hands of the Soviets.

A painting by V. Serov on the central wall depicts Lenin addressing the Second All-Russia Congress of Soviets. Arranged below the picture are the first legislative acts adopted by the Soviet state: the Decree on Peace, the Decree on Land, and the decision to form a Soviet government–the Council of People's Commissars headed by Lenin. Also displayed here is the "Declaration of the Rights of the Peoples of Russia" which the Soviet government passed on November 2, 1917. The Declaration proclaimed the basic principles of Lenin's national policy adopted by the Soviet state–equality and sovereignty for all the nationalities of Russia, their right to free self-determination, including the right to secede, and abolition of all national and religious privileges and restrictions.

The revolution's gains were consolidated in the "Declaration of Rights of the Toiling and Exploited People" adopted by the Third All-Russia Congress of Soviets in January 1918. Lenin's manuscript of this fundamental document, which served as the basis for the first Soviet Constitution, is on display.

The final section of the room is devoted to the international significance of the Great October Socialist Revolution of 1917, the most important event of the 20th century.

The Socialist Revolution in Russia opened up a new era in the history of mankind: the collapse of capitalism and the establishment of a new, socialist society. Lenin's prediction that the 1917 October Revolution would be of significance not only to Russia, but to the whole world has been borne out by history. The ideals of October 1917 are a great transformatory force in modern history.

СВОБОДА
СВОБОДНАЯ РОССІЯ
СВОБОДА
АРМІЯ

FIRST FLOOR

ROOMS NOS 11-23

Days of the Revolution. Voskressenskaya Ploshchad, March 2. Lithograph, 1917.

FOUNDER OF THE FIRST SOCIALIST STATE (OCTOBER 1917-1918)

The collection in Room 11 is devoted to the titanic work done by Lenin in the first year of Soviet power when the world's first state of workers and peasants was being created.

The display opens with a quotation from Lenin, "Soviet power is the road to socialism that was discovered by the masses of the working people, and that is why it is the true road, that is why it is invincible."

The 1917 Socialist Revolution awakened broad masses of the working population to active political life. In power for the first time, the Bolshevik Party was faced with the complex task of creating a new society whose main purpose was to protect the workers' vital interests. This task could be accomplished only by the masses themselves.

On November 5, 1917 Lenin wrote a message, "To the Population" in which he said,

"Comrades, working people! Remember that now *you yourselves* are at the helm of state. No one will help you if you yourselves do not unite and take into *your* hands *all affairs* of the state. *Your* Soviets are from now on the organs of state authority, legislative bodies with full powers."

Lenin's manuscript of the message is on the wall left of the entrance in the centre of the section devoted to the building up of a new state apparatus. At the time, this task had become a priority, and "an arch-difficult thing to accomplish", as Lenin put it. Among the workers and peasants there was no one qualified for the job: quite naturally, they had no experience in governing the state. The difficulties were made still greater by the fact that part of the intelligentsia and some high-ranking officials who had worked for the old regime disrupted the work of the new government in every way they could. In addition, the country's economy, backward as it was, had been further undermined by the war.

However, Lenin had total confidence in the creative energy of the masses. Having freed themselves from exploitation and social injustice, they could commit all their strength, enthusiasm and initiative to the cause of building a new society. History was to prove Lenin right. The workers and peasants played an active part in the fight to eliminate capitalism and build socialism in Russia. And, while the construction of a Soviet socialist state was in progress, they gradually acquired the skills of governing.

As part of their programme to eliminate the bourgeois and landlord-dominated state, administrative machinery and to create a new state apparatus, the Soviet government passed a number of decrees: on the abolition of social estates and civil ranks, on courts, on the separation of church from state and of schools from the church and others. The decrees are displayed in show-cases together with Lenin's manuscript of "The Declaration of Rights of the Toiling and Exploited People". This document laid down the main tasks to be fulfilled by Soviet power: all exploiters' resistance suppressed, society organized along socialist lines, and an end put to the division of society into classes. This historical document was later added as an Introduction to the Constitution of the RSFSR, the first fundamental law of Soviet Russia devised with Lenin's active participation.

The next section is dedicated to the building up of the Soviet Republic's defence, the Party's struggle to achieve the country's withdrawal from the imperialist war, and the conclusion of a universal peace. The section is prefaced with a quotation from Lenin,

"No revolution is worth anything unless it can defend itself."

On January 28, 1918 the Soviet government issued a decree which instituted the Red Army of Workers and Peasants. At first the Red Army's recruits were volunteers and came solely from among the working classes. The decree with Lenin's amendments is displayed in a stand along with a photograph showing the enlistment of the volunteers. The first Soviet soldiers were sent to the most dangerous parts of the front

Lenin attending a meeting of the Council of People's Commissars at Smolny. 1918.

near Pskov, Reval (now Tallinn) and Narva where fierce fighting began to contain the German army units.

Above this stand to the left of the entrance is one of the first Soviet posters, *Have You Volunteered?* Its dynamic, bold outlines make a strong impact. Other political posters are displayed in the following rooms. In those years such posters laconic and expressive in style with clear, striking captions were an effective form of propaganda.

There are documents reflecting the uncompromising struggle which Lenin and the Party waged to withdraw the country from the war. In this they were opposed by the Trotskyists and "Left Communists"* who maintained that peace with Germany would disrupt the revolutionary movement in the West and lead to the restoration of bourgeois rule in Russia. Lenin, for his part, stressed that by opposing the moves towards peace, they jeopardized the very existence of the Soviet Republic.

Displayed in a show-case are "The Revolutionary Phrase" and "Strange and Monstrous", two articles which Lenin wrote in February 1918 when the Party was bitterly divided over whether to sign a peace treaty, to which Germany agreed, on very harsh terms for the Soviet Republic. Lenin realized though that the absence of a peace treaty amounted to a death warrant for Soviet power. And therefore with his usual courage and consistency he stuck to his course for peace on the proposed terms. The peace treaty, which was finally signed in the Byelorussian town of Brest-Litovsk on March 3, 1918[1], became known as the Brest-Litovsk Peace Treaty.

Peace with Germany gave the workers' and peasants' republic

---

[1] From now on all dates are given according to the Gregorian calendar.

the respite it badly needed. The Soviet people were now able to concentrate all their material and spiritual resources on the restoration of the national economy ruined by war and on the other tasks of the Socialist Revolution.

In April 1918, Lenin wrote "The Immediate Tasks of the Soviet Government". The first edition of this work is prominently displayed in the centre of another wall of the room, together with photocopies of pages from the original manuscript. In "The Immediate Tasks" Lenin outlines a plan for socialist construction and the main course that Soviet economic policy should take. He also reveals the main problems facing the country now it had entered a period of transition from capitalism to socialism.

The following quotation from Lenin, mounted on the wall, sums up his idea of the Party's main objective following the victory of the October 1917 Revolution:

"We, the Bolshevik Party, have *convinced* Russia. We have *won* Russia from the rich for the poor, from the exploiters for the working people. Now we must *administer* Russia."

The socialist construction began in a complex situation. By the summer of 1918, a severe food problem had arisen. The imperialist military intervention and a number of counter-revolutionary revolts cut off Central Russia from the main wheat-producing areas—the Ukraine, the Volga area and Siberia. The kulaks, or rich farmers, hid their wheat and refused to sell it to the state at fixed prices. The workers in Moscow, Petrograd and other cities went without food rations for weeks while the peasants in many areas were starving.

It was at this time that Lenin wrote that now the main thing is the fight for food because the fight for food is equivalent to the fight for socialism. The Party and government took a whole series of measures to eliminate the famine and supply the population with food. Teams of workers were sent to the countryside with authorisation to buy grain. A campaign was launched against the black marketeers speculating in grain. All wheat and flour stocks and supplies of bread were put under strict control. The exhibits in this section include Lenin's appeal to the working people, "Comrade workers! We are going to fight our last and decisive battle!", a letter "On Famine" addressed to the Petrograd workers, and a photograph, "A Workers' Food Requisitioning Team Setting Off for the Countryside. 1918."

The exhibits on the wall opposite the entrance are devoted to the Soviet government's first steps in cultural construction. In January 1918, two months after the Revolution, Lenin addressed the Third All-Russia Congress of Soviets with the words:

"In the old days, human genius, the brain of man, created only to give some the benefits of technology and culture, and to deprive others of the bare necessities, education and development. From now on all the marvels of science and the gains of culture belong to the nation as a whole, and never again will man's brain and human genius be used for oppression and exploitation." This quotation forms part of the exhibition.

Speaking at the 1st All-Russia Congress on Education in August 1918, Lenin sets the task of bringing up the rising generation to become conscious and active builders of socialism. A photocopy of his speech is displayed on a stand together with decrees on wiping out illiteracy among the adult population and on opening the workers' faculties.* Another exhibit in the stand is the manuscript of a draft resolution on People's Commissars' Council ruling on the admission of workers' and peasants' children as students at colleges and universities in the Russian Republic. Thus the land of the Soviets set to work to create an intelligentsia.

A prominent place in the room is given to the Constitution of the RSFSR* which was drawn up with Lenin's active participation. On display in a special stand are the Soviet Republic's State Emblem and the text of the Constitution

State Emblem of the Russian Socialist Federative Soviet Republic. 1918.

Пролетаріи всѣх странъ соединяйтесь".

Н. ЛЕНИН.

ОЧЕРЕДНЫЯ ЗАДАЧИ СОВѢТСКОЙ ВЛАСТИ.

МОСКВА.

Cover of "The Immediate Tasks of the Soviet Government". 1918.

(The Fundamental Law of the Russian Soviet Federative Socialist Republic) approved by the Fifth All-Russia Congress of Soviets in July 1918. This was an act giving legal sanction to the basic gains of the October Revolution of 1917: the establishment of workers' and peasants' political power, the transfer of the main means of production into the hands of the people, and the establishment of genuine democracy for the broadest masses of the people. The Constitution gave all the working people equal economic and political rights. Supported by the broad working masses, Soviet power was confidently gaining ground.

... Shortly before the October Revolution, the monarchic newspaper *Novoye Vremya* (New Times) wrote,

"Allow us to think for a moment, that the Bolsheviks are victorious. Who will govern us then? Cooks, experts in cutlets and steaks? Or firemen? Stable-men, stokers? Or perhaps nannies will run to the meeting of the Council of State between diaper washing?

Lenin in his study in the Kremlin. October 16, 1918.

Who, then? Who are these statesmen? Perhaps locksmiths will take care of theatres, plumbers of diplomacy and carpenters of the post and telegraph?... Will this come to pass? Is this possible? No! History shall provide the Bolsheviks with the answer to this crazy question."

History provided the answer to this question in the very first months of Soviet power when the working people proved themselves capable of tackling major affairs of state, managing the economy and creating a new culture. For the first time in world history the working class succeeded both in taking over power and in keeping a firm grip of it.

A show-case in the room contains documents illustrating Lenin's activity in devising principles of government and improvements in the style of Party and government work.

Engrossed as he was in his titanic work, Lenin nevertheless found time to worry about the health of his comrades. On view is a note (one of many) he wrote to A. D. Tsyurupa, "Dear A. D.! You are becoming absolutely impossible in your treatment of government property.[1]

"Your prescription is three weeks treatment! And obey Lidiya Alexandrovna* who will send you to a sanatorium.

"It is utterly unpardonable to waste away your health which is poor. You must be made well!" In the summer of 1918, the People's Commissar for Food, A. D. Tsyurupa, who worked himself to exhaustion every day, had a breakdown. This was noticed by Lenin who saw that the Commissar looked ill and tired, and obviously needed a rest and medical treatment.

Two special glass cases in the

[1] Lenin here refers half-jokingly to human health.

middle of the room display the overcoat and jacket Lenin wore on August 30, 1918 when he spoke at a rally at the Michelson Works (now the Vladimir Ilyich Factory). As he was leaving the factory building, a terrorist Fanny Kaplan shot and seriously wounded him. A show-case in the last section of the room displays letters and telegrams sent to Lenin by workers, peasants and Red Army men expressing concern and affection and wishing their leader a speedy recovery.

Being a man of strong physique Lenin soon recovered, and on September 16 he was back at his desk again. However, his daily workload proved too much of a strain and on the insistence of his doctors he went to the village of Gorki outside Moscow to rest. A photograph in the collection shows the room in a former Manor House in Gorki in which Lenin lived in September and October 1918. It was here that he wrote the greater part of his work, *The Proletarian Revolution and the Renegade Kautsky*. Some of the pages from the original manuscript are on display. *The Renegade Kautsky* was written in response to Karl Kautsky's articles against the Russian Communist Party. A particular target for Lenin's biting criticism was Kautsky's book *On the Dictatorship of the Proletariat* which openly attacked Marxism and the socialist revolution in Russia. In *The Renegade Kautsky* Lenin denounces Kautsky's revisionist attitude and the treacherous stance he had adopted, his confused theoretical premises, and his misrepresentation of Marxism on the questions of bourgeois and proletarian democracy. Lenin also demonstrates the world-wide significance of the experience the Communist Party and Soviet government were acquiring in building a society upholding the interests of the working people.

The following quotation from *The Renegade Kautsky*, mounted in large letters, forms part of the exhibition: "Proletarian democracy is a *million times* more democratic than any bourgeois democracy; Soviet power is a million times more democratic than the most democratic bourgeois republic."

Room No. 12

ORGANIZER OF THE SOVIET REPUBLIC'S DEFENCE: (1918-1920)

In the summer of 1918, the Soviet Republic was surrounded on nearly all sides by hostile armies. Three-fourths of its territory was occupied by foreign interventionists and internal counter-revolutionary forces. The country's desperate plight is illustrated by a map.

The peaceful respite which followed the Brest Treaty proved all too short. In March 1918, the first units of British, American and French troops landed at Murmansk, a Russian city on the Barents Sea. In April, Japanese and American troops seized the Pacific port of Vladivostok. Photographs in the collection show Americans landing at Vladivostok and British soldiers marching through the streets of Archangel.

At the end of May, the Volga area, the Urals and a big part of Siberia were occupied by the Czechoslovak Corps. Formed before the Revolution from Czech

Have You Volunteered? Poster by D. Moor. 1920.

and Slovak P.O.W.s (formerly soldiers of the Austro-Hungarian army) to fight against Germany, the Corps was incited by the Entente* agents and assisted by the Czech anti-Soviet leaders, to rebel against the Soviet Republic. In violation of the Brest Peace Treaty, units of the German Army seized the Baltic provinces, Byelorussia and the Ukraine. The Soviet people were forced to take up arms.

The foreign intervention and Civil War in Russia lasted for more than two years (1918-1920). During these years, Lenin showed himself to be not only a leader of a new type of state, but also a remarkable strategist with a profound knowledge of the art of war. On exhibition are his letters and telegrams to commanders of fronts and armies, and verbatim reports of his speeches at rallies, meetings, congresses, and conferences in which he explains the situation in the country, sets forth urgent tasks, and calls on his audiences to do everything for the front, for victory. I. Grabar conveys the strain of Lenin's everyday work in his painting, *Lenin on the Direct Line*. The Soviet leader was in constant touch with military commanders at the front. The poster, *Soviet Russia—a Camp under Siege. All Hands to the Defence!*, is displayed left of the first window in the room. On the same wall hangs a picture, *Long Live the Three-Million-Strong Red Army*, executed in the style of the popular Russian print.

The tremendous efforts to mobilize the country's forces to defeat the enemy soon brought tangible results. In the autumn of 1918, the Red Army won its first victories over the interventionists and White Guards. The mortal danger to the Soviet Republic was eliminated. It was against this background that the Soviet people celebrated the first anniversary of the Revolution. On the eve of the celebration the Sixth All-Russia Congress of Soviets held its sessions. The Congress was addressed by Lenin whose speech was dedicated to the 1st anniversary of the Revolution and to the successes scored by the working people in building a new life. The preparatory notes for his speech are on display. The next day Lenin made a speech at the unveiling ceremony of a temporary monument to Karl Marx and Friedrich Engels in Voskresenskaya (now Revolution) Square, in the centre of Moscow. After the

Lenin speaking at the unveiling ceremony of a temporary monument to Marx and Engels. Moscow. November 7, 1918.

Cover of the *Programme of the Russian Communist Party (Bolsheviks)* adopted at the Eighth Congress, 1919

РОССИЙСКАЯ КОММУНИСТИЧЕСКАЯ ПАРТИЯ (большевиков).

Пролетарии всех стран, соединяйтесь!

ПРОГРАММА

РОССИЙСКОЙ КОММУНИСТИЧЕСКОЙ ПАРТИИ

(БОЛЬШЕВИКОВ).

Принята 8-м съездом партии 18—23 марта 1919 г.

Цена 1 рубль.

Книгоиздательство „КОММУНИСТ".

МОСКВА | ПЕТРОГРАД

МОСКВА - 1919.

ceremony, Lenin walked with a group of demonstrators to Red Square where he made another speech at the unveiling ceremony of a plaque in memory of the heroes of the October Revolution. Many photographs in this section show Lenin animated and happy. His wife, Nadezhda Krupskaya, later recalled that he smiled all the time and that the days when the first anniversary of the Revolution was celebrated were the happiest in his life.

Lenin often warned that the war was not yet over, that the enemy was still strong, and that a bitter struggle lay ahead. A number of exhibits are devoted to the introduction of the so-called "war communism" under which all major, middle-sized, and small industries were nationalized, universal labour service introduced, food supplies rationed, private trade banned and the peasants had to sell all their surplus produce to the state at fixed prices. War communism was a harsh measure forced on the Soviet Republic by war, economic ruin and the scarcity of food supplies. Subsequent developments showed that in that situation this was the only proper policy which could ensure victory in the Civil War.

The numerous exhibits arranged on the walls between the windows are devoted to Lenin's efforts to create a third Communist International. Among them are photographs and documents showing the growth of the revolutionary movement in the capitalist countries due to the influence of the October Revolution. Communist parties were set up in a number of countries. Consistently adhering to the principles of proletarian internationalism, the Russian Communist Party (Bolsheviks) and the Soviet government did everything they could to help the peoples who were fighting for their freedom.

When the revolution broke out in Germany in the autumn of 1918, Lenin wrote in a note (on display on the central wall),

"Let us all die but help the German workers in their cause of advancing the revolution in Germany. Conclusion: 1) let us increase tenfold our efforts to obtain more food (*all* reserves should be put to use, both for us and *for the German workers*)..."

Lenin worked for several years to unite the left-wing elements in the Socialist parties and to create the Third Communist International (Comintern). Early in March 1919, 52 delegates from 30 countries gathered in Moscow for the first congress of the International convened at his initiative. There are photographs and other documents in the room relating to this major event which inscribed a new page in the history of the world-wide Communist movement at a time when the revolutionary process was in the ascendant. Lenin addressed Congress delegates with a report, "Theses on Bourgeois Democracy and the Dictatorship of the Proletariat", in which he proved

Lenin inspecting the *Vsevobuch* units on Red Square. May 25, 1919.

that the dictatorship of the proletariat was essential for the exercise of power by the working people and for the transition from capitalism to socialism.

The Congress formally announced the establishment of the Third Communist International. It also approved Lenin's report and adopted a manifesto appealing to the workers of the world. Summing up the results of the Congress, Lenin said that whereas the First International had laid the foundations of the working-class revolutionary movement, the Third International set out to translate the dictatorship of the proletariat into practice.

The items exhibited on the central wall are devoted to the work of the Eighth Congress of the Russian Communist Party (Bolsheviks) in March 1919. The Congress delegates approved a new Party Programme whose principal sections were drawn up by Lenin. A stand displays proofs of the Programme with Lenin's corrections, and also the original manuscript of several of its clauses. The new Programme laid down a set of tasks for the period of transition from capitalism to socialism. Soviet government was to be consolidated throughout the country, and industry and agriculture developed, with the state owning all means of production and the entire national economy built up according to a general plan. Productivity of labour was to be raised, and the masses were to play a more active part in achieving these tasks. In agriculture the Programme envisaged the implementation of socialist reform by organizing co-operative and state farms. Much space in the Programme was devoted to the need to raise the material well-being and cultural level of the working people.

The second Party Programme adopted at the Eighth Congress of the Russian Communist Party was of world-wide, historical significance—the first programme of a Communist party in power, it outlined the tasks involved and the course to be followed in building a socialist society.

As the Congress was drawing to a close, a report came in that the counter-revolutionary armies and interventionist troops had launched a major new offensive. The Soviet Republic was again in danger. More than a million workers and peasants united in a single force to repulse the enemy. The offensive began from every direction at once—from north, south, east and west. The military operations in 1919 are marked on a map which forms part of the collection.

Among the exhibits in this section are "Theses of the Central Committee of the Russian Communist Party (Bolsheviks) on the Situation on the Eastern Front", a Party Central Committee letter, "All Out for the Fight Against Denikin", sent out to all Party organizations, and other similar documents mobilizing the Party and people to fight the enemy. In these appeals, Lenin called on the workers to do their job selflessly, with revolutionary ardour so as to meet the needs of the front and crush the interventionist and White Guard armies. The workers responded by holding Communist *subbotniks** throughout the country. In his article, "A Great Beginning" (some pages from the article are on display) Lenin praised this initiative launched by the Soviet workers. He described the *subbotnik* campaign as the first actual beginning of communism. The voluntary work in free time marked the beginning of a communist attitude to labour.

Thanks to the tremendous efforts of the Party, and the dedication with which the workers did their jobs, the Red Army soon had everything it needed. It launched an offensive against the counter-revolutionary troops and foreign interventionists, and before long, won a number of crucial battles, which decided the outcome of the Civil War.

On display are photographs of prominent military leaders and political workers in the Red Army—Mikhail Frunze, Ivan Fedko, Vasili Chapayev, Nikolai Shchors, Kliment Voroshilov, Felix Dzerzhinsky, Sergei Kirov, Valerian Kuibyshev and others. There are other photographs of the foreign internationalists who fought to defend the Soviet Republic—Mihai Bujor (Romania), Jaroslav Hašek (Czechoslovakia), Oleco Dundič (Yugoslavia), Béla Kun (Hungary), Jeanne Labourbe (France), Paou Ti-san (China), John Reed (United States), and Karol Świerczewski (Poland). Thousands of other internationalists fought in the battles for Soviet power, and many of them gave their lives for it...

Visitors to the room can see a short documentary, *Lenin as Leader of the Soviet Republic's Defence*. Also on view are the presents Lenin received from Red Army soldiers and commanders—an army overcoat with the red toggle loops, a holster, two Budyonny army caps and top boots.

The exhibits also include a number of honorary revolutionary banners which the Soviet government awarded to the Red Army units who excelled themselves in fighting the enemy. Another item is a scale model of Armoured Train No. 6 named after Lenin. The train covered thousands of miles during the Civil War and took part in defeating the interventionist and White Guard troops.

Despite the intervention and Civil War, requiring so much of his time and attention, Lenin kept up his theoretical studies. He gave much of his attention to the problems of socialist construction. Nadezhda Krupskaya recalled,

"Ilyich's (Lenin's) ability to study theory at the most critical point of struggle always amazed me; he searched for the solution of practical questions in theory."

A number of show-cases in the room display Lenin's theoretical works of this period, such as "On the Dictatorship of the Proletariat" and "The Economics and Politics in the Era of the Dictatorship of the Proletariat". He further advances the Marxist teaching about the transition from capitalism to socialism and outlines ways to solve the crucial problems of the socialist construction.

Room No. 13

THE END OF FOREIGN INTERVENTION AND CIVIL WAR

After the main forces of the counter-revolutionaries and foreign interventionists were routed early in 1920, the Soviet Republic had another peaceful respite which it badly needed to heal the grievous wounds inflicted by the war. The country was in a shambles. Fuel was in short supply, and there was not enough food. Considerable effort and self-sacrifice were needed to restore the economy. At Lenin's suggestion the government set up a State Commission for the Electrification of Russia, or GOELRO which was to devise a plan to restore and develop the economy on the basis of electrification. Some two hundred experts were asked to work on the plan. In Lenin's view, the GOELRO project was to secure Russia's economic independence and create a new technological base and major modern industries. The work of the GOELRO Commission is reflected in the items displayed in the room.

Late in March and early in April 1920, the RCP(B) held its Ninth

Lenin. July 1920.

Congress. Displayed in a showcase are Lenin's "Letter to the Organisations of the Russian Communist Party (Bolsheviks) [RCP(B)] on the Preparation for the Party Congress", a Central Committee report to the Congress written and delivered by Lenin, the Congress ruling on an integrated economic plan, a Congress delegate questionnaire filled in by Lenin, and a number of other exhibits.

Of particular interest is a questionnaire which Lenin filled in on September 17, 1920 during the re-registration of members affiliated to the Moscow RCP(B) branch. The 45 answers he gave show how modest and unassuming he was. Answering one of the questions, "What languages (apart from Russian) do you speak, read and write?" he wrote, "French, German and English, all of them poorly." In fact, Lenin knew several languages. He could read and write English, French and German, in which languages he addressed Comintern Congresses and conversed with foreign delegations. He could also read Polish and Italian, and understood Swedish and Czech.

Another characteristic answer is to the question, "What form did your participation in the October Revolution take?" Lenin wrote "Member of the Central Committee", stressing that the Committee took decisions collectively. Lenin regarded collective leadership to be the most important principle on a party and government level, one to which he strictly adhered in all his work.

"Lenin's personality is a harmonious combination of leader and individual a glorious destiny, as Karl Marx put it, for the fighter for Communism," wrote Clara Zetkin, the prominent German and international Communist leader.

A large part of the exhibits mounted on the walls between the windows feature Lenin's book *"Left-Wing" Communism—an Infantile Disorder* and materials on the Second Congress of the Comintern. The first edition of *"Left-Wing" Communism*, written in April and May 1920, is given pride of place. In stands nearby are translations of the work. In *"Left-Wing" Communism* Lenin sums up the revolutionary experience of the Russian Bolsheviks and the international working-class movement. Proceeding from this experience he works out the strategy and tactics to be adopted by Communist parties at a time of general crisis for capitalism and when two socio-political systems confront each other on the world scene.

Lenin levelled sharp criticism at the so-called Left-Wing Communists who called for an all-out offensive without taking into consideration the specific political conditions of the moment. He demonstrated the futility of the Left-Wing Communists' tactics which could lead to the defeat of the Communist movement. He called for an uncompromising struggle against any sort of opportunism and revisionism as being extremely harmful to international Communist unity. He urged the Communists of the world to master every form of revolutionary struggle and to work hard to

Cover of *"Left-Wing" Communism—an Infantile Disorder*, 1920.

win over the broad masses of the workers to the side of Communism. He wrote, "Communists should know that, in any case, the future belongs to them." *"Left-Wing" Communism*, which was published on the eve of the Congress, was tremendously important for the Comintern's ideological and organizational unity.

Lenin's book is still topical. It is often published and re-printed in different countries. As of January 1, 1986 it has appeared in the Soviet Union in 63 languages in more than 13,2 million copies.

The Second Congress of the Comintern opened on July 19, 1920 in Petrograd and resumed work on July 23 in Moscow. A blow-up mounted on the central wall of the room shows Lenin delivering a Report on the International Situation and the Fundamental Tasks of the Communist International at a meeting of the Second Congress (July 19, 1920). Other exhibits there include a verbatim record of the report with Lenin's amendments as well as drafts of major decisions taken by the Congress. In his speeches at the Congress, Lenin gave a detailed analysis of the international economic and political situation following the proletarian Revolution in Russia. He wrote that World War I and the Revolution had set off a general crisis of capitalism. He outlined the specific features of the crisis: the division of the world into socialist and capitalist systems, the increasingly acute economic contradictions and class struggle in the capitalist world, and the crisis which had hit the imperialist colonial system. The 1917 Revolution in Russia gave a powerful impetus to the national liberation movements in China, India, Indonesia and the other colonial countries. Lenin closely followed these developments and regarded them as being of great importance. At the Congress he put forward a draft resolution on the national liberation movement. The thesis he advanced was that the backward countries which had shaken off the imperialist yoke can, with help from the socialist countries, make the transfer to socialism, by-passing the capitalist stage of development.

The peaceful respite did not last long. At the end of April 1920 the troops of bourgeois Poland invaded the Ukraine and seized Kiev. The former tsarist general Wrangel, who was entrenched in the Crimea, launched an offensive against the Donbas coalfield, from which came most of Russia's coal. His other objective was the Kuban area, the country's granary. Lenin said, "... we say that we are not defending the right to plunder other nations, but are defending our proletarian revolution, and will defend it to the very end. The Russia which has been emancipated and which for two years had borne untold suffering for the sake of her Soviet revolution–that Russia we shall defend to our last drop of blood!"

A map indicates actions taken on Lenin's instructions to defend the country in 1918-1920. On the map is a quotation from Lenin,

"It was only because of the Party's vigilance and its strict discipline, because the authority of the Party united all government departments and institutions, because the slogans issued by the Central Committee were adopted by tens, hundreds, thousands and finally millions of people as one man, because incredible sacrifices were made–it was only because of all this that the miracle which occurred was made possible."

The Civil War and foreign intervention ended in complete victory for the Red Army. The telegram exhibited in this section was sent by Mikhail Frunze, Commander of the Southern Front, to Lenin, "Today our cavalry has taken Kerch. The Southern Front has ceased to exist." It was sent on November 16, 1920.

The final section in the room deals with the establishment of Soviet power in Azerbaijan, Armenia and Georgia which were ruled by nationalist governments. The working people in the Caucasus rose up in arms and, overthrowing these governments, proclaimed Soviet power. In his letters, Xerox copies of which are on display, Lenin welcomed the three new Soviet republics in the Caucasus. He said he was confident "... that their close alliance will serve as a model of national peace, unprecedented under the bourgeoisie and impossible under the capitalist system". At the same time Lenin warned the Communists in the three Transcaucasian republics against copying the methods used in the fight for Soviet power in Central Rus-

Lenin at the Second Congress of the Communist International. 1920.

sia. He spoke of the need to take into account local conditions and make concessions to the peasants who made up an overwhelming majority of the population.

A replica of Lenin's study in the Kremlin can be seen in a room off Room 13. The furniture is unpretentious—a desk, a wooden armchair with a wicker-work back and seat, a table placed so as to form a single top with the desk, armchairs for the visitors and a sofa. To the right and left of the desk are revolving bookshelves. They held materials relating to Party Congresses, conferences and Congresses of Soviets, reference books, dictionaries, and folders containing various papers which Lenin needed for his work, as well as Russian and foreign newspapers.

Standing between the windows are bookcases which contained nearly two thousand books. Most of Lenin's library was kept in the room adjoining the Soviet government's reception room. In his library in the Kremlin Lenin had a total of over ten thousand books, magazines and other publications, with a thousand books in English, French, German and other languages. They included works by Marx, Engels, Plekhanov, Lafargue, Bebel, Mehring and Rosa Luxemburg, as well as philosophical writings by Hegel, Feuerbach, Campanella, and Saint-Simon. Some of the books were by the Russian revolutionary democrats Hertzen, Belinsky, Chernyshevsky, Dobrolyubov and Pisarev. There were a lot of works on history, political economy, the economics of Russia and the world, the natural sciences, philosophy, engineering, military subjects, and the other sciences. Russian and world fiction was also represented. In the study are many maps and atlases which Lenin constantly used in his work. Hanging over the sofa is a portrait of Marx given to Lenin by workers from Petrograd and a bas-relief portrait of Stepan Khalturin.* Lenin was so accustomed to his small, cosy study that he refused all suggestions to move into a more spacious room.

His working day began very early and lasted late into the night. Here, in his study he worked on plans for socialist construction and directed the country's defence effort during the Civil War and foreign intervention. There he received prominent Communist and working-class leaders and met workers, peasant deputies sent by villages in various gubernias and with proletarian intellectuals. His conversations with these visitors provided Lenin with valuable authentic information for his plans for socialist construction.

One of the doors of the study opened into a corridor, another into a "box", or switch-board, and a third into the conference room of the government, the Council of People's Commissars or Sovnarkom. Adjoining the Sovnarkom conference room at the end of a corridor was the flat in which Lenin and Krupskaya lived. A scale model of it can be seen in Room No. 15.

In the corridor between Rooms Nos. 13 and 14 stands a Rolls Royce (No. 236), which Lenin used in 1922-1923.

LEADER IN PEACEFUL SOCIALIST CONSTRUCTION

Room No. 14 is dedicated to Lenin's work in the last few months of 1920 when the main forces of the counter-revolution and foreign interventionists had been defeated, and the Soviet people started to restore the war-ravaged industry and agriculture and to build socialism.

The grave situation in the country is illustrated by the tables displayed in the room.

In a situation like this it was hard to believe that it would ever be possible to restore the economy let alone to get socialist construction off the ground. However, Lenin looked boldly into the future. He firmly believed that socialism would eventually triumph. He advanced the idea that Russia should be transferred to large-scale use of electricity. His formula containing this idea, "Communism is Soviet power plus the electrification of the whole country" is inscribed in large letters on the central wall of Room 14 as the motto of the display.

One of the photographs on view shows Lenin talking to H. G. Wells on October 6, 1920 when work on the GOELRO project was in full swing. For all Wells' vision of the future mankind, he found it hard to foresee Russia's immediate future. He dismissed Lenin's plan as "the Utopia of the electrification". In his *Russia in the Shadows* he wrote,

"Can one imagine a more courageous project in a vast flat land of forests and illiterate peasants, with no technical skill available, and with trade and industry at the last gasp?... I cannot see anything of the sort happening in this dark crystal of Russia, but this little man at the Kremlin can; he sees the decaying railways replaced by a new electric transport, sees new road ways spreading throughout the land, sees a new and happier Communist industrialism arising again."

Some of the exhibits—documents and other materials—reflect the discussions at the Eighth All-Russia Congress of Soviets, held at the Bolshoi Theatre, in Moscow, in December 1920. At Lenin's suggestion, the GOELRO project was put on the Congress agenda. Lenin delivered a major report on the work done by the VTsIK* and the Council of People's Commissars. As Chairman of the GOELRO Commission, G. M. Krzhizhanovsky spoke on the electrification project. The delegates who had come from various parts of the devastated country, were poorly dressed and hungry. Sitting in the cold and dimly lit auditorium at the Bolshoi, they listened with bated breath to the daring prospects for socialist construction in their land. The artist L. Shmatko has captured this atmosphere in his painting, *Lenin by the GOELRO Map. The Eighth All-Russia Congress of Soviets.* December 1920.*

The delegates unanimously voted for the project. In their resolution they expressed confidence that the workers and peasants "would exert every effort and shrink from no sacrifice to carry out the plan for the electrification of Russia at all costs, and despite all obstacles".

On a stand is a photograph showing Lenin and his wife, Nadezhda Krupskaya, with the peasants of Kashino, a village near Moscow, on November 14, 1920. They went there to attend the ceremony for the opening of a power station built with the money of an agricultural co-operative. In one of the houses, Lenin spoke with the villagers, and to mark the occasion he and Krupskaya were later photographed with them.

After this, Lenin spoke at a rally.

Other photographs in the room are of the first thermal power stations built under the GOELRO project. Among the exhibits is a scale model of a hydroelectric project on the Volkhov River in the Leningrad region. The 66,000-kw station was commissioned in 1926. This was an encouraging beginning. The toiling people in Soviet Russia saw for themselves that the GOELRO project could be accomplished.

The letters, telegrams and documents displayed on the wall between the windows reflect Lenin's day-to-day work: his direction of the construction of power stations and efforts to restore and develop heavy industry and agriculture.

The closing section of the display is dedicated to the Third Congress of the Young Communist League, or Komsomol. Pride of place here is given to the first published edition of a speech, "The Tasks of the Youth Leagues", which Lenin made at the Congress in October 1920. A painting by P. Byelousov shows Lenin standing amidst delegates to the Congress.

Lenin and H.G.Wells. Moscow. October 6, 1920.

* * *

The documents, photographs and other items on display in Room 15 are dedicated to the major events in the Soviet Union in 1921-22. The exhibits left of the entrance and between the windows feature Lenin's preparations to launch the New Economic Policy, or NEP, forced on the country by life itself.

In the first few months of 1921 the economic difficulties facing Russia grew worse. The peasants had become even poorer as a result of a series of bad harvests, shortages of fodder and an outbreak of cattle plague. Food supplies in the cities had diminished. Lack of fuel brought to a halt the industries which had been restored after the war. In various parts of the country the kulaks stirred up anti-Soviet unrest among the peasants whose discontent with War Communism, particularly with grain requisitioning,* had reached its peak.

The central exhibit on the wall on the left is the "Rough Draft of Theses Concerning the Peasants" in which Lenin formulates key measures designed to replace grain requisitioning by a tax in kind. The "Rough Draft" is based on a detailed analysis of the state of the country's economy and on Lenin's personal observations. As part of his study of the conditions of peasants' life in Russia, Lenin visited a number of villages in the Moscow Province. He also received peasants from Central Russia and Siberia in the Kremlin, and carefully read the letters they sent him. It was obvious that the requisitioning of grain made necessary by the Civil War needed to be replaced by a clearly defined tax in kind, allowing the peasants to dispose of their produce as they wished once the tax had been paid.

Lenin's "Rough Draft" which outlined the transition to the NEP policy was the main item put forward for discussion at the forthcoming Tenth Party Congress.

The Party's course towards peaceful socialist construction was obstructed by the Trotskyites, the Workers' Opposition, the Democratic-Centralists group and other opportunist factions. They were united by their disbelief in the triumph of socialism, and they rejected the Communist Party's leading role in socialist construction. They imposed on the Party a debate on the trade unions. The Trotskyites insisted on the introduction of military methods in the unions, which meant the use of coercion in order to involve the workers in socialist construction. They also sought to turn the unions into government bodies. The "Workers' Opposition", on the other hand, advocated anarcho-syndicalist views. They demanded that the trade unions should be put in charge of managing industry.

Room No. 15

Lenin speaking at the Third Congress of the Communist International held in the Kremlin. 1921.

Lenin sitting on the presidium rostrum steps at the Third Congress of the Communist International.

On view are manuscripts and first editions of Lenin's articles, "The Trade Unions, the Present Situation and Trotsky's Mistakes", "Once Again on the Trade Unions, the Current Situation and the Mistakes of Trotsky and Bukharin" and "The Party Crisis" in which he demonstrates that the position taken by the factionalists was ideologically weak and essentially anti-Marxist. He describes Trotsky's views as theoretically erroneous and politically harmful.

The debates that followed revealed that a majority of the Party organizations rejected the views and demands of the opposition and favoured Lenin's line. The opposition was utterly defeated, and the Party consolidated its positions. The Party policies were supported by the broad working masses.

The next section of the display relates to the Tenth Party Congress in March 1921. Among the exhibits are a photograph of Lenin speaking at the Tenth Congress in the Sverdlov Hall in the Kremlin, his report on the RCP(B)'s political activities, and statements on the replacement of the requisitioning of grain by a tax in kind, on Party unity and anarcho-syndicalist deviation. There are also manuscripts of the drafts of the major decisions taken at the Congress. The Congress decided that requisitioning should be abolished in favour of a tax in kind. This decision was taken in the interests of the toiling peasants. It provided the incentive to expand the area of land under crops, improve farming methods, and raise productivity.

The Congress condemned the various factions within the Party, showed that their views were untenable, and called for a constant and uncompromising fight against them. It passed a resolution, "On Party Unity" which stipulated that all factionalist groupings had to be disbanded. Failure to comply entailed immediate expulsion from the Party. This resolution, a copy of which is displayed on a stand, provided the Party with a guideline in the struggle for the preservation of Party unity and for the consolidation of its ranks.

The documents and other items on show in the room testify to Lenin's unflagging theoretical and practical work. No detail escaped his attention. He tackled Party and government leadership, and the restoration and advancement of industry, agriculture, science, education and culture.

Just how hard Lenin worked can be seen from the following list of matters he attended to on February 2, 1921, an ordinary workday:

Took the chair at a Council of People's Commissars meeting on the organization of communications between all the People's Commissariats with responsibility for the economy;

Read a telegram dated 1st February 1921, from Omsk, signed by I. N. Smirnov, Chairman of the Siberian Revolutionary Committee, concerning the deteriorating situation in Siberia and the stepping up of terrorist attacks;

Attended a Politbureau meeting of the Central Committee of the Russian (Bolshevik) Communist Party;

Dictated a telegram to the Petrograd provincial committee concerning the decision to buy 18,5 million poods of coal abroad for provision to Petrograd;

Read a draft decree of the Politbureau of the Central Committee of the Russian (Bolshevik) Communist Party concerning the provision of aid to peasants who had suffered from the bad harvest;

Signed draft Council of Labour and Defence* resolutions on:

the provision of food supplies to the Donbas area, measures to increase mining and deliveries of coal, provision of fuel to Petrograd, the calling to account of those guilty of delay in despatching telegrams with the Council of Labour and Defence resolutions on procurement and deliveries of fuel and other matters.

Signed an All-Russia Central Executive Committee and Council of People's Commissars' draft resolution on transferring to the courts of law all cases of desertion from the armed forces and a Council of People's Commissars' draft resolution on the Polish prisoners of war.

Talked on the telephone with M. K. Vladimirov, People's Commissar for Food in the Ukraine;

Despatched the following books to D. B. Ryazanov, Director of the K. Marx and F. Engels Institute: *F. Engels. Political Testament. From the Unpublished Letters,* (Berlin 1920) and *A Collection of Articles, Excerpts and Documents,* edited by Ye. Dran in honour of the centenary of Engels' birth, (Vienna 1920). In an accompanying letter Lenin asks Ryazanov to let him know whether it is possible to buy abroad originals (or photocopies) of the unpublished letters of the founders of Marxism, to collect in Moscow all published writings of Marx and Engels; whether a catalogue of those of their works and papers already available in Moscow has been compiled, whether the letters of the founders of Marxism are being collected.

Sent a letter to A. B. Goykhbarg, deputy chairman of the Narrow Council of People's Commissars*, in which he underlines the urgency of the housing question in Moscow, suggests a check should be kept how flats are distributed, indicates the need for permanent control over the number of employees in the People's Commissariats.

Wrote a note to E. A. Preobrazhensky, Commission member of the Central Committee of the Russian (Bolshevik) Communist Party on the reorganization of the People's Commissariat for Education.

Took the chair at a Russian (Bolshevik) Communist Party Central Committee Commission meeting on the reorganization of the People's Commissariat for Education.

Talked to V. N. Sokolov, representative of the People's Commissariat for Land in Siberia and member of the Siberian Revolutionary Committee* about the situation in the Siberian contryside following the introduction of the requisitioning of farm produce, and listened to his suggestions for possible changes in the form of requisitioning and that peasants be given the right to dispose of surplus grain.

Received G. M. Krzhizhanovsky, Chairman of the State Commission for Electrification of Russia.

Read a letter (in English) from L. Bryant, the American journalist, in which she informs Lenin that two books by John Reed, writer, publicist and prominent figure in the American working-class movement, have been sent to him.

Wrote answers to notes from his secretary.

Conducted negotiations over the telephone with the leaders of the People's Commissariats and departments on various questions relating to socialist construction.

Despite his colossal workload, whenever he could Lenin found time to help the people he met. Displayed in one of the show-cases is a photocopy of a letter he wrote to the People's Commissar of Health, N. A. Semashko, following his meeting with I. A. Chekunov, a peasant from the Vladimir Province. While they were talking, Lenin noticed that his guest had poor eye-sight. It turned out that the man had bought poor quality spectacles after having lost his own. In his note to N. A. Semashko, Lenin wrote, "I have here with me Comrade Ivan Afanasievich *Chekunov*, a very interesting and hardworking peasant, who promotes the Communist principles in his own way.

"He has lost his spectacles and paid 15,000 roubles[1] for a *piece of trash.* Could you help him get good spectacles? Please help him, and ask your secretary to tell me what you have been able to do."

Testing the first Soviet-made electric plow near Moscow. October, 1921.

A large section of the room is dedicated to the Third Congress of the Comintern, held in June-July 1921. In the centre of the display is a photograph of Lenin addressing the Congress plus photographs of delegates representing foreign Communist parties—Paul Vaillant-Couturier and Marcel Cachin (France), Vasil Kolarov and Georgi Dimitrov (Bulgaria), Béla Kun (Hungary), Ernst Thälmann and Clara Zetkin (Germany), William Gallacher and Thomas Bell (Britain), Bohumír Šmeral (Czechoslovakia) and others.

The Congress discussed the world Communist and working-class movement and considered Comintern strategy and tactics. In his report on RCP(B) tactics (a copy of the manuscript can be

[1] As per the exchange rate for those years.

seen in a stand) Lenin explained the New Economic Policy to delegates and analysed the alignment of class forces in the world arena. He pointed out that international imperialism had proved itself unable to overthrow Soviet power in Russia by military means, that the world Communist movement had gained momentum, and that the fight against imperialism conducted by peoples in colonial and semi-colonial countries was expanding. He also noted that in a number of countries the revolutionary action taken by the proletariat in 1920-1921 had been defeated, that the bourgeoisie had launched an offensive against the working class, and that the revolutionary movement in these countries was on the wane. The Communist parties had to take all these factors into account in their activities. The new conditions required a decisive change in the tactics of the revolutionary struggle.

On display in the room is a verbatim report of Lenin's speech in which he supports the Comintern's tactics. Here also are the original letters he wrote to the Polish and German Communists in which he substantiates the tactics for a united front, tactics for winning the trust and confidence of the masses.

Lenin talking to P. P. Christiansen of the US Farmers' and Workers' Party. Kremlin. November, 1921.

One of the last sections in the room is devoted to Lenin's guidance of Soviet foreign policy based, from the very first days of the October Revolution, on the principle of peaceful coexistence between states with different socio-political systems.

Among the items on view in the section are the peace treaties which Soviet Russia concluded with Estonia, Latvia, Lithuania,* Poland, Finland, Mongolia, Persia, Turkey and Afghanistan early in the 1920s. The treaties ensured the successful development of friendly and good-neighbourly relations with these countries in different spheres of life.

A number of documents are dedicated to preparations for and the meetings of an international economic conference in Genoa, in April 1922. Although Lenin was chosen Chairman of the Soviet delegation, the burden of affairs of state and his health made it impossible for him to go to Italy. However, he wrote directives and sent letters and telegrams to the head of the Soviet delegation, G.V. Chicherin, giving detailed instructions on the strategy and tactics to be followed by Russia's representatives at the Conference.

In Lenin's view, the Soviet delegation had to work towards two aims: (a) the achievement of peace and economic co-operation between nations and (b) the establishment of business and trade relations with the capitalist countries. The major point in the Soviet declaration at Genoa was a proposal on the universal reduction of armaments.

During the Conference, Soviet Russia and Germany signed a treaty in the town of Rapallo, near Genoa. The Treaty (a copy of which is among the exhibits) envisages the restoration of diplomatic relations between the two countries and the expansion of mutually advantageous economic relations.

The last section in the room is devoted to the 11th Congress of the RCP(B) held in March and April, 1922. The exhibits include Lenin's draft manuscript for a RCP(B) Central Committee report, copies of speeches made at the closing session and pages from the Congress bulletin. In the report Lenin summed up the results of the first year under NEP. NEP had fully justified itself, since it had created political and economic conditions favourable for the construction of the material and technological base of socialism.

The last items in the room are materials relating to the Fourth Comintern Congress, the last congress to be attended by Lenin. On November 13, 1922 he addressed Congress delegates with a report, "Five Years of the Russian Revolution and the Prospects of the World Revolution". Drafts of the report are on display including a copy in German. A list of the relief funds and supplies sent to Soviet Russia by workers from all over the world is given in the following table:

France—nearly 1 mln francs;

Czechoslovakia—7.5 mln korunas and 2 mln korunas worth of food;

Germany—1.3 mln marks and 1 mln marks worth of food;

Holland—100,000 guldens;

Italy—nearly 1 mln lire;

Norway—100,000 kroner;

Austria—3 mln kronen;

Spain—50,000 marks;

Poland—9 mln Polish marks;

Denmark—500,000 marks.

The sculptural portraits of Lenin in the room are by N. Andreyev. The painting, *Lenin on the Rostrum*, is by A. Gerasimov.

LENIN: FOUNDER OF THE SOVIET UNION (1922)

In the five years since its foundation the Soviet republic had strengthened its positions. First successes were scored in the restoration of the economy and in the implementation of the GOELRO project. The first thermal and hydroelectric power stations had been built. The working people's living standards had been improved in town and countryside. On November 7, the day of the anniversary, the working people staged rallies and demonstrations throughout the country to express their determination to build a new society free from exploitation.

A show-case displays an issue of *Pravda* carrying Lenin's speech at the plenum of the Moscow Soviet on November 20, 1922. In his speech Lenin expresses confidence that the Party could succeed in solving its main task that of building socialism. He said,

"Difficult as this task may be, new as it may be compared with our previous task, and numerous as the difficulties may be that it entails, we shall all—not in a day, but in a few years—all of us together fulfil it whatever the cost, so the NEP Russia will become socialist Russia."

The items arranged on the central wall illustrate the formation of the Union of Soviet Socialist Republics (USSR). A facsimile of a quotation from Lenin on the wall reads,

"We want a *voluntary* union of nations—a union which precludes any coercion of one nation by another—a union founded on complete confidence, on a clear recognition of brotherly unity, on absolutely voluntary consent."

Other exhibits on view are the Treaties which the Russian Federative Republic signed with other Soviet republics—the Ukraine, Byelorussia and the Transcaucasian Federation and the decrees which the government of Soviet Russia adopted on assistance to other republics in the restoration of their economies and in socialist construction. On the wall is a manuscript of Lenin's "Theses for the Second Congress of the Communist International. Rough Draft of the Theses on National and Colonial Questions" (1920). In it the Soviet leader emphasized how important it was for the independent Soviet republics to unite into a single state.

In the first place, he writes, in view of the capitalist encirclement, it is impossible to sustain the existence of the Soviet republics without the closest union between them.

In the second place, it is impossible to restore the means of production destroyed by imperialism and to ensure the well-being of the working people without a close economic union between the Soviet republics.

In the third place, such a union would make it possible to set up a single planned socialist economy.

Other items on display include numerous letters and resolutions passed at meetings of the working masses held in cities and the countryside which express a firm determination to become united into a single state. There are also decisions taken by Congresses of the Soviet republics to the effect that the establishment of a Union of Soviet Republics is both desirable and necessary. Giving expression to the will of all the nations and nationalities, the First All-Union Congress of Soviets approved on December 30, 1922 in Moscow, the Declaration and Treaty on the Formation of the Union of Soviet Socialist Republics.

Following the Congress, the Presidium of the USSR Central Executive Committee issued an address to all the nations and governments of the world. The address, a copy of which is on view, proclaims,

"The union state, which has been created ... on the basis of fraternal co-operation between the peoples of the Soviet republics sets itself the aim of living in peace with all nations. Acting and working together in harmony the equal nationalities will develop their culture and prosperity and fulfil the tasks of the working people's power."

THE LAST YEAR OF LENIN'S LIFE AND WORK (DECEMBER 1922-JANUARY 1924)

The titanic workload involved in Lenin's leadership of the Party and state and the aftereffects of the attempt on his life undermined his health. In December 1922, he had an attack which led to a sharp deterioration in his condition. The doctors forbade him to do any work or read newspapers and magazines. He insisted, however, on dictating his "diary". On view is a photocopy of a register kept by secretaries on duty who recorded all the work did between December 23, 1922 and February 9, 1923. The following works were dictated by Lenin over this period: "Letter to the Congress", "On Granting Legislative Functions to the State Planning Commission", "The Question of Nationalities or 'Autonomisation'", "Pages from a Diary", "On Co-operation," "Our Revolution", "How We Should Reorganise the Workers' and Peasants' Inspection" (Recommendation to the 12th Party Congress), and "Better Fewer, but Better". Pages from these works form part of the display.

Although he was severely ill, Lenin retained a clear mind and immense will-power and was highly optimistic. "He was a very cheerful, persistent and steadfast person, an optimist. His usual, predominant mood was one of intense concentration," Nadezhda Krupskaya wrote later. His work on his last letters and articles required really heroic efforts: already seriously ill, at first he was only able to dictate for five to ten minutes per day, and later for no more than 30 to 40 minutes a day. This entailed great difficulties. Lenin was in a hurry to express everything on his mind. Besides, he was not accustomed to working with a stenographer. Before his illness, he had written most of

Lenin at Gorki. August 1922.

his letters and articles himself. He said that he was used to seeing his manuscript before his eyes, to stopping and considering in the difficult cases when he "got stuck", walking about the room, even simply running out to take a walk; and now he often wanted to grab a pencil and make his corrections himself. Dictating was an additional strain. First he had to turn his ideas over in his mind so as not to waste a moment in dictation. But, with his usual persistence he overcame all difficulties. "He dictates splendidly as he always does, without stopping, rarely having to search for the appropriate form of expression. Indeed, rather than dictating, he speaks and gesticulates," a secretary on duty wrote in the register on February 2.

Lenin's indomitable willpower, the awareness of his responsibilities and his concern for the future of his country and its further development gave him the strength to overcome pain and to accomplish what seemed to be beyond human capacity. Despite his illness, he wrote a number of remarkable works in a mere six weeks. As is the case with all his work, they are distinguished by clear, profound thought, impeccable logic and excellent knowledge of life.

Room No. 18

HALL OF MOURNING

Lenin died in Gorki not far from Moscow at 6.50 p.m. on 21 January 1924, three months before his 54th birthday. The next day an extraordinary plenary session of the RCP(B) Central Committee adopted an appeal, "To the Party. To All Working People."

The wall to the right of the entrance is painted black. Against this background is an excerpt from the appeal,

"All that is indeed great and heroic in the proletariat—the fearless mind, the iron, inflexible, persistent will that overcomes all obstacles, the sacred hate, the hate for slavery and oppression till death, the revolutionary fervour which can move mountains, the boundless faith in the creative forces of the masses, the vast organizational genius—all this found its personification in Lenin, whose name became the symbol for the new world from the East to the West, from the North to the South."

A few hours after Lenin's death, his death mask and casts of his hands were made by the sculptor, S. Merkurov. They are in the centre of the exposition. Next to them are wreaths and banners. Hanging on the wall, which is made to imitate the wall of the Kremlin, are photographs showing people paying their last respects to the Soviet leader.

On January 27, 1924, at 16.00 Moscow time, Lenin's body was laid to rest in the Mausoleum to the sounds of funerary music, thousands of factory hooters, and an artillery salute.

During the days that followed Lenin's death, more than 240 thousand workers joined the Communist Party. Some of the applications for membership are displayed in show-cases. In another case are letters and telegrams of condolences received from Soviet citizens and from people abroad.

The room contains photographs of the temporary wooden Mausoleum where Lenin's body was placed on 27 January, and the scale model of the present Mausoleum in marble and granite. An endless file of people have been coming here for more than half a century.

... We are in Red Square. It is very nearly 11 o'clock in the morning. The doors to Lenin's Mausoleum will soon open. The square is filled with sunshine: sentries, their bayonets gleaming, guard the black-and-red granite Mausoleum.

The Kremlin clock chimes the hour. With firm measured step the sentries change guard. As the chimes fade away, the doors of the Mausoleum open. The people queueing outside enter it and walk down the steps into the Hall of Mourning. Lenin lies in state in a glass sarcophagus in the middle of the Hall. Each visitor sees him for a total of eighty seconds: an eighty seconds that will remain with them for the rest of their lives.

Lenin's funeral. Moscow, January 1924.

Room No. 19

A GREAT HERITAGE OF IDEAS

The heritage of ideas left by Lenin is the subject of the display in Room 19 in which are exhibited various editions of his works published both in this country and abroad. The first of Lenin's known works was published in 1893 and his last in 1923. Within a space of thirty years Lenin wrote hundreds of books, thousands of articles and letters and made innumerable reports. As of today, over 21 thousand of his works and other documents have been published.

On display in the room is every edition of Lenin's *Collected Works* ever published in the USSR. The first edition was printed at the decision of the Ninth Party Congress while Lenin was still alive. In 20 volumes, it contains more than 1,500 works.

In a show-case is the Central Committee decision dated 8 January 1957 to publish Lenin's Complete Works in 55 volumes. The first volumes of this last edition, which comprises some nine thousand works and documents, were issued in 1958 and Volume 55 in 1965. About 1,100 works are published for the first time.

Among the other items on view are anthologies, selected works, and separate editions of his books and articles published in the Union republics in Russian and in the vernacular languages. As of 1 July 1985 the total number of copies of works by Lenin published in the USSR in the 68 languages of this country and in 54 foreign languages stood at over 622 million.

Lenin's momentous ideas are treasured by working people throughout the world. Hundreds of red signs on a large globe in the middle of the room mark the cities and countries where Lenin's works have been published. Lenin's works head the list of most widely translated literature.

The exhibits include an anthology of Lenin's works published in 1919 in Budapest in Hungarian under the title, *The Path of Struggle*. It contains "Letters on Tactics", "The April Theses", and his speeches at the Third Congress of the Soviets. In 1919, the Bulgarian Communists set up Liberation, a workers' co-operative, with a publishing department which was to produce and distribute Marxist literature. In 1922, Liberation printed a pamphlet containing Lenin's article, "The Importance of Gold Now and After the Complete Victory of Socialism", and other papers. In the years of fascist reaction, Lenin's *"Left-Wing Communism"* was published illegally by the German Communists. It was distributed as a manual on travelling and athletics. Defying a repressive police regime, the Argentinian Communists issued a 43-volume Spanish-language edition of Lenin's complete works in an impressive total of 276 thousand copies. Copies of all these editions are represented in the collection.

Lenin's works are regularly published in over fifty foreign countries: Britain, the United States, France, Brazil, Italy, Sweden, Finland, India, Czechoslovakia, Poland, Bulgaria, and Vietnam, to name but a few. Some of these editions are displayed together with a jubilee 12-volume edition of Lenin's works printed in Japan to mark the 90th anniversary of his birth. In the post-war years, two-volume collections of Lenin's works have been issued in New York, Athens, Milan, Oslo, Brussels, Tokyo and other places. All in all, his articles and books have been published in 134 languages in various countries.

The friezes decorating the walls of Room 19 illustrate the significance of Leninism for working people in the Soviet Union building the road to communism, for the peoples building socialism in their own countries, and for those who are fighting for the victory of democracy and socialist revolution or support the establishment and consolidation of independent national states.

Room No. 20

LENIN'S PLAN TO BUILD SOCIALISM IN THE USSR TRANSLATED INTO PRACTICE (1925-1941)

The documents, photographs, and scale models of machines and buildings in the collection reflect the construction of socialism in the USSR in the years between 1925 and June 1941.On the central wall is a quotation from the new edition of the Programme of the Communist Party of the Soviet Union: "The working man became the sole master of the country. A socialist society was built in the USSR." This is the result of a social revolution of worldwide historical significance.

Displayed in stands and showcases are excerpts from the Marxist-Leninist classics on the role of the proletarian dictatorship in socialist construction. Also on view is the Chapter on Economic Tasks from the Party's Programme adopted at the RCP(B)'s Eighth Congress in March 1919. Prominently inscribed is a quotation from the CPSU Programme on the key items of Lenin's plan for the construction of socialism in the USSR–socialist industrialization, the organization of the peasants into farming co-operatives, and the cultural revolution. Show-cases contain the following and other works by Lenin on these subjects: "The State and the Revolution", "The Immediate Tasks of the Soviet Government", "Economics and Politics in the Era of the Dictatorship of the Proletariat", "Better Fewer, But Better", "On Co-operation".

The exhibition is divided into four main sections. Section One is a documentary story illustrating the implementation of Lenin's plan for industrialization.

The Soviet method of industrialisation differed radically from the capitalist method. Capitalist countries obtained the means they required for this purpose from intense exploitation of the workers, by imposing war indemnities, plundering colonies and making use of foreign loans. Such methods were out of the question in the case of the Soviet Union, which relied on its own resources to industrialize: profits from nationalized industries, savings accumulated from agriculture and from domestic and foreign trade earnings. The economy drive was the order of the day. One of the items on view is an appeal issued by the Central Committee of the All-Union Communist Party (Bolsheviks), "On the Economy Drive. To All Party Organizations, To All Party Control Commissions, To All Party Members Employed by Productive, Co-operative, Commercial, Banking and Other Establishments". Another item is an application submitted to the Central Committee of the Textile Workers' Union by women workers from the Krasny Perekop Factory, in Yaroslavl, who asked to be given four looms to operate instead of two. This document is one of many showing that public ownership of the means of production and the interest every worker took in the successful operation of the economy had become a reliable guarantee of the feasibility of all targeted plans.

During the first five-year plan of 1929-1932, which was fulfilled ahead of schedule, the state was able to spend 8.8 thousand million roubles in capital investment, or twice the sum spent in the previous (1918-1928) decade. In the second five-year plan of 1933-1937, capital investment shot up to 19.7 thousand million roubles. In the three and a half years of the third plan up to the time Nazi Germany attacked the Soviet Union in 1941, capital investment amounted to 20.4 thousand million. These figures are illustrated in a chart, "Capital Investment in the USSR (in comparable prices)".

A powerful industry was in the making in the USSR. New factories, big for those days, were under construction, such as the Urals Engineering Plant, the Magnitogorsk Steel Mill and the Gorky Motorworks. The construction of these projects is the subject of photographs on the walls. Special issues of *Pravda* newspaper carrying the following headlines—"Ural-Kuznetsk Complex—Triumph for Party Line", "Five-Year Plan Creates Thousands of Industries", "USSR Ploughs Fields with Its Own Tractors and Drives Its Own Cars" and

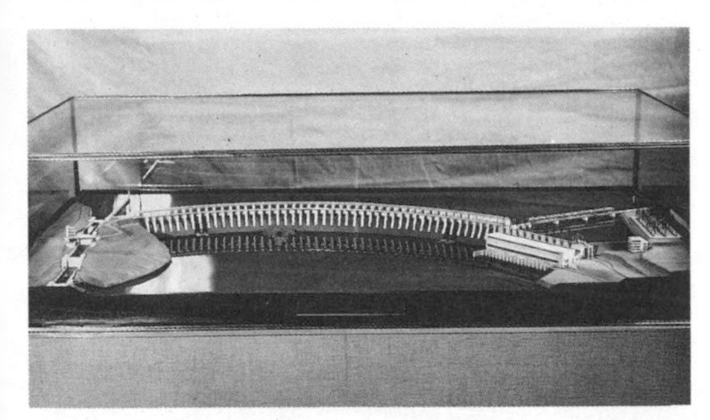

Mock-up of the Dnieper Hydroelectric Power Station, the first Soviet power station (1932).

others—reflect the successes scored in industrialisation in those years.

Some of the exhibits tell the story of the Dnieper Hydroelectric Power Station, the first major project of the first five-year plan. This station, forming part of the GOELRO project, was originally called Alexandrovskaya after I. G. Alexandrov who designed it. Alexandrov told Lenin that the complex development of Zaporozhye, one of the richest areas in the Ukraine, offered vast potential. This could be achieved by building a powerful electric station on the Dnieper River rapids. "I am your sincere supporter," Lenin told Alexandrov. "To tell you a secret, we must have abundant imagination, we must be able to dream while remaining arch-realists."

The whole country took part in building the project, the biggest in Europe. Its first phase generated 650 thousand kilowatts. Exhibits relating to the power station form part of the display: a Council of Labour and Defence ruling "On Construction of the Dnieper Power Station" passed in 1921, with Lenin's participation, a scale model of the construction site, and a photograph of the rally held to inaugurate the V. I. Lenin Dnieper Station in 1932.

Early in the 1930s factories and plants were built in every republic. The photographs in the room show the ceremony for the opening of the Turkestan-Siberian Railway in 1930, an overall view of the May Day Dam across the Zeravshan River in the Uzbek SSR (1930) and a panorama of the Bukhta Ilyicha oilfield in Baku (1935). A table of statistics on the wall indicates that in comparison with 1913, gross industrial output by 1940 had grown by: 324 times in Tajikistan, 153 times in Kirghizia, 68 times in Azerbaijan and 23 times in Armenia. The modern industry being built up in every constituent republic was tremendously important in the efforts to eliminate backwardness and ensure the all-round development of formerly oppressed peoples.

The success of socialist industrialization aroused a great surge of enthusiasm among millions of people who now showed a new, creative interest in their work. Among the exhibits is a bas-relief presented to the Museum by workers from the city of Kharkov bearing the following inscription: "Five-Year Plan in Four Years." Employees in many industries displayed an exemplary attitude to their work.

In a stand between the windows on the left is a copy of Lenin's article, "How to Organize Competition?", which was published posthumously in *Pravda* in January 1929. Prominence is given to the following excerpt from the text, "Far from extinguishing competition, socialism, on the contrary, for the first time creates the opportunity for employing it on a really *wide* and a really *mass* scale ..."

In another stand between the windows there is a special display for a photostat of the first Soviet agreement for a socialist emulation drive. In 1929, a cutters' team from the pipe shop at the Krasny Vyborzhets Factory in Leningrad challenged the working force of all plants and factories in the USSR to compete against each other in increasing their production quotas. Many took up the challenge.

A significant page in the chronicles of the socialist emulation campaign was inscribed by the Stakhanovite movement. In 1935 Alexei Stakhanov, a peasant turned miner, produced 102 tons of coal in one shift, 14 times his daily quota. He had quite a few followers, many of whom worked at enterprises other than mines. A 1935 photograph in the room shows Alexei Stakhanov explaining his system of operation to workers at the Irmino colliery.

In the years between 1928 and 1941, this country built nine thousand new industrial enterprises as is shown on a map, "Projects in the First Five-Year Plans" mounted in the middle of the room. The success of the industrialisation campaign was an impressive achievement for a nation which had started from scratch.

The second section in the display is devoted to the socialist transformation of agriculture, a programme devised by Lenin and implemented by the Party and the Soviet people. The following works by Lenin are on display: the original version of his article, "The Immediate Tasks of the Soviet Government", "Draft of RCP(B) Programme", "Report on Work in the Countryside, 23 March 1919", "The Tax in Kind", "On Co-operation" and others. These works outline ways along which peasants could embark on socialist production. They spell out the basic principles and forms of co-operative farming. Another item on view is a resolution, "On Work in the Countryside" passed in December 1927, by the Party's 15th Congress which has become known as the Collectivisation Congress. Among the other exhibits in the section are several Party documents dedicated to socialist reform in the countryside.

This was an immense task. A diagram in a show-case shows that there were 24 million small peasant farms in the countryside. The peasants were a large and mostly backward mass of people. Without a radical reorganization of the peasant class into co-operatives, the plan to build socialism was inconceivable. The Communist Party, therefore, attached great importance to propaganda of the experience gained by this country's first co-operative farms set up under Lenin's direct guidance. The peasants had to be convinced of the advantages of

Young women of Turkmenia, who have shed the yashmak, are learning to read and write.

collective farming over individual farming. A photograph shows the Soviet President Mikhail Kalinin handing over an act granting land in perpetual tenure to the Sotsialdy collective farm, in the Kazakh Republic, in 1935.

Exhibits testify to the considerable help given by the working class to the peasants. Lenin had once dreamed of one hundred thousand tractors being supplied to the countryside. A number of diagrams show that whereas in 1928 there were 18 thousand tractors in the countryside, by 1940 this number had risen to 684 thousand. Several photographs show the welcome given to the first tractor in the village of Larino near Smolensk in 1925; the sowing of crops at the Gigant collective farm in the Northern Caucasus in 1930; tractors at the Krasny Putilovets Factory in Leningrad in 1929; and the mass application for collective-farm membership in the Borisoglebsky district, in Central Russia, in 1930. A scale model of the first Soviet wheel tractor of 1930 is also displayed in the room.

The collectivisation of agriculture went on successfully. By the mid-30s, collective and state-owned farms had become dominant in the countryside. The emergence of collective farming as the basis of a large-scale socialist crop-growing economy converted the Soviet Union from a country dominated by a mass of petty peasant farmsteads into a land of major mechanized agriculture.

The third section of the room is dedicated to the enormous transformations that took place in Soviet culture. The following quotation from Lenin is prominently displayed:

"Education workers, and the Communist Party as the vanguard in the struggle, should consider it their fundamental task to help enlighten and instruct the working masses."

A number of diagrams, tables and photographs illustrate how illiteracy was eliminated and secondary education built up, cultural and educational offices established, and how a new intelligentsia dedicated to the people's cause emerged. They also speak of the achievements in Soviet science, of the efforts to bring up a new man, and of the genuine cultural revolution that took place throughout the USSR including such formerly remote provinces of Russia as Central Asia, the Far North and Siberia.

The Table "Growth in Number of Universities, Colleges and Technical Schools in the Constituent Republics" indicates the importance attached to the training of qualified specialists. Whereas in 1914-1915, there was not one college or university in Kazakhstan and Central Asia, by 1941 there were 67 establishments of higher education in these regions.

As part of the cultural revolution, the Soviet state sought to ensure genuine equality of rights for women in the USSR. A 1925 photograph in one of the stands shows young Turkmenian women, who had just discarded their yashmaks, sitting in a classroom. The photograph is symbolic of the tremendous effort that had to be made to combat women's backward position in formerly remote provinces where century-old traditions still dominated the minds and everyday life. Education helped millions of women of various nationalities to contribute to socialized production and to take part in the country's political and cultural life. By 1940, women made up 41 per cent of all Soviet industrial and office employees, this figure having grown three fold as against the late twenties.

The final section of the display shows the changes that had taken place in Soviet society. From the documents, tables and diagrams on view it becomes clear that by the mid-30s, socialist relations in production had been established in all parts of the national economy and that a new socialist economy had been set up. The socialist revolution had accomplished its main task. From now on the working class, peasants and intelligentsia determined the pattern of Soviet society.

A stand and show-case right of the entrance contain exhibits relating to the Leninist policy on nationalities adopted by the Soviet state. The documents on display illustrate the growth of industry and development of culture in the constituent republics. There are materials about the accession of Lithuania, Latvia, and Estonia to the Soviet Union, about the proclamation of the Moldavian Soviet Socialist Republic, and other developments.

In 1936, the Soviet Union adopted a new Constitution which gave legislative expression to the victory of socialism in the country. The Constitution is among the exhibits in the room.

At the end of the display is a quotation from Lenin:

"A socialist Soviet Republic in Russia will stand as a living example to the peoples of all countries, and the propaganda and the revolutionizing effect of this example will be immense."

DEFENDING THE ACHIEVEMENTS OF SOCIALISM DURING THE GREAT PATRIOTIC WAR (1941-1945)

Two documents—one dated 21 February 1918 and the other 29 June 1941—are on display: Lenin's decree, "The Socialist Fatherland Is in Danger", and a directive jointly issued by the Council of People's Commissars and by the All-Union Communist Party (Bolsheviks) Central Committee to all Party and state organizations in the front-line areas. There is a direct link between the two documents: at times of danger for the nation, the Communist Party and Soviet government appeal to the people to take up arms to fight the enemy.

The famous poster *Your Motherland-Country Is Calling* by I. Toidze hangs on the central wall. The exhibits include a copy of *Pravda* for 3 July 1941 with a speech by Stalin, Chairman of the State Defence Committee, and two photographs: one shows an infantry column marching to the front in June 1941, and the other—the military parade in Moscow on 7 November 1941.

The month of November was cold and snowy in that first year of the war. Leaving a trail of footprints in the wet snow behind them, Soviet soldiers clad in army coats and carrying combat arms marched past Lenin's Tomb, in Red Square. From Red Square they went straight to the front to block Hitler's approach to Moscow.

"Every time a difficult situation arose during the war the Party mobilised the Communists," Lenin wrote during the Civil War. This quotation is given prominence in the display. During the Great Patriotic War every other soldier was a Communist or a Komsomol member. The Communists who fought in the most dangerous or difficult parts of the front were model fighters whose courage, military tactics and selfless devotion to Lenin's cause served as an example to others. "We are defending Lenin's cause. There can be no doubt that the enemy will be defeated. We shall win," wrote Communist soldiers in one of their combat news releases in December 1941.

Stands and show-cases contain precious mementoes of the war years—Party and Komsomol membership cards stained with blood and riddled with enemy bullets, applications for Party membership which Red Army soldiers and commanders wrote during lulls in the fighting, soil from Mamayev Hill soaked with the blood of the defenders of Stalingrad, newspapers produced by underground Party committees in the Nazi-held territory, and oaths sworn by partisans and signed in their blood.

The Party was in charge of put-

Victory Parade. June 24, 1945.

Soldier-liberator. Sculptor Ye. Vuchetich.

ting the economy on to a war footing. In a large-scale operation carried out with the minimum of delay, the Soviet people successfully moved industrial enterprises to the eastern parts of the country. As a result of heroic efforts, within three or four weeks the resited factories and plants were operating round the clock to make everything needed for the front. Among the exhibits in the room are samples of weapons this country made during the war, as well as banners awarded to the working force of various industrial enterprises and to combat units on behalf of the State Defence Committee. Other awards on display are Soviet medals and orders.

On display is a copy of the statue of Lenin sculpted by M. Manizer in 1926. This sculpture has an interesting history. In 1935, the Bronze-Casting Works in Leningrad cast a bronze copy of the statue for the town of Pushkin near Leningrad. When they occupied Pushkin in October 1943 the Germans sent the statue to the town of Eisleben in Germany to be melted down. However, an anti-Nazi group managed to save it and on 2 July 1945, it was installed in one of the squares in Eisleben.

Among the exhibits are donations the Museum has received from abroad. A bas-relief of Lenin was presented by the Communist cell in the town of Romainville in France. It bears the inscription: "This is the work of Comrade Marcel Ethis shot by the Nazis in Mont-Valérien on 11 August for sheltering the patriots." A kerchief with Lenin's portrait was donated by the Edmond Devaux Communist cell. The kerchief belonged to a Communist, Edmond Devaux, whom the Nazis put before a firing squad for his anti-fascist activities.

Another donation comes from Spain. It is a small photograph of Lenin in Red Square on 7 November 1919. The Spanish Communist poet, Marcos Ana, who sent the photo, recalls that this picture of Lenin helped him and his comrades to endure the tortures they were subjected to in the fascist prison of Porlier.

The just war of liberation against the Nazis ended in victory. The Soviet Army rescued the peoples of Europe from slavery and delivered the Asian nations from the Japanese imperialist yoke. Some of the photographs in the room show the welcome which the Soviet soldiers were given in Poland and Romania, in Czechoslovakia and Bulgaria, in Hungary and Yugoslavia, in North-Western China and in Northern Korea.

A large photograph depicts the Victory Parade on June 24, 1945. The victorious soldiers who have saved the world from the fascist scourge march through Red Square, carrying standards with black eagles and swastikas, emblems of the Nazi divisions and regiments they have routed. They throw them down onto the cobblestones at the foot of Lenin's Mausoleum.

The following quotation from Lenin inscribed in large letters forms part of the exhibition:

"A nation in which the majority of workers and peasants realise, feel and see that they are fighting for their own Soviet power, for the rule of the working people, for the cause whose victory will ensure them and their children all the benefits of culture, of all that has been created by human labour—such a nation can never be vanquished."

The last section of the display reflects the efforts made by the Party and state to consolidate the country's defences and strengthen its armed forces today. A number of photographs show the military manoeuvres held by the Warsaw Treaty armies and meetings between soldiers from the Soviet Union and other socialist states. The Soviet Army is a reliable guard of the Soviet Union's security and a protector of peace.

Room No. 22

THE PERFECTION OF SOCIALIST SOCIETY AND THE BUILDING OF COMMUNISM

The display in the room begins with documentary and other materials illustrating the efforts to restore the war-ravaged Soviet economy. Left of the entrance is a table, "The Damage the Nazi Invaders Inflicted on the National Economy". More than twenty million Soviet citizens died at the front and in Nazi concentration camps. One-third of the country's wealth was destroyed. On Soviet soil, the Nazis burnt and left in ruins 1,710 cities and towns, more than 70 thousand villages, and tens of thousands of industrial enterprises, hospitals, secondary and technical schools, colleges, universities and libraries. Photographs in this section show Leningrad in ruins (1943) and other Soviet cities, towns and villages after being sacked by the Nazis.

One of the documents on view is "The Law on the Five-Year Plan

The first rehabilitated blast furnace at the Zaporozhstal Works (1947).

for the Restoration and Development of the USSR National Economy in 1946-1950". In that five-year plan, the first to be adopted by the USSR Supreme Soviet after the war, the main economic and political goal was not merely to restore industry and agriculture to their pre-war capacity, but also to raise the economy to a much higher level. The plan was accomplished in four years and 3 months. In the first stand inside the entrance, there is a selection of copies of *Pravda* carrying articles about the socialist emulation drives launched throughout the country to fulfil production quotas in industry ahead of schedule. Displayed next is a medal, "For the Restoration of Ferrous Metallurgy Plants in the South" instituted by the government in 1948. In World War II the Soviet Union lost 68 per cent of its industrial plants producing cast and pig-iron and 58 per cent of its steel industry. The major iron and steel mills in the south of the USSR were destroyed by the Germans who invaded the area. Restoration of these industries was a priority which was tackled immediately after the Germans were expelled in 1943.

As a result of hard work and self-sacrifice, the first furnaces went back into operation early in 1945. The medal, "For the Restoration of Ferrous Metallurgy Plants", was awarded to more than 68 thousand people. Next to the medal is a scale model of the first furnace to be restored at the Zaporozhstal Works in 1947.

Displayed on the stands are Party Congress decrees setting out basic principles of the development of socialism into communism.

Exhibited alongside the original draft copies of articles by Lenin, "The Immediate Tasks of Soviet Power", and other works on the construction of socialism, is the present-day Party Programme adopted at the 27th Congress of the Communist Party of the Soviet Union. This is a programme for the systematic and all-round perfection of the socialist system that has achieved total victory in the USSR, for Soviet society's further advance to communism on the basis of the country's socio-economic development. This is a programme for the struggle for peace.

"In the name of man, for the good of man", these are the words inscribed on the banner of socialist society, as is illustrated by the exhibits in the room. In this society: exploitation has been got rid of forever; conditions have been created for improving the welfare of the whole people; an equal right to work is guaranteed and national inequality has been eliminated; genuine democracy is developing and a genuinely humanist Marxist-Leninist ideology predominates; finally, a socialist way of life has taken shape giving the working man confidence in the future.

At the present stage of perfecting socialism, the creative forces of the new system and the advantages of the socialist way of life are coming into their own. A powerful industry is at work in the country, our scientists and artists lead the world.

The Communist Party of the Soviet Union and the Soviet state pay particular attention to the development of the economy as being an all-important condition for the construction of the new society. On display are the basic guidelines adopted by the congresses for the economic and social development of the USSR over five-year and longer periods.

Party policy today is aimed at speeding up the socio-economic development of the country. Many exhibits in the room illustrate this goal: they testify to the radical modernization of industry and agriculture thanks to the achievements of science and engineering and show the Party line as being to raise the national economy to an entirely new scientific and technological level.

Today, special attention is given to power engineering, metallurgy and machine-building. One of the tables on display, "Production of Major Types of Industrial Output", shows that whereas in 1940 gross output of electricity was 48.6 thousand million kilowatt-hours and in 1980 it stood at 1,295 thousand million, by the end of the 11th five-year plan period it was more than 1,550 thousand million kilowatt-hours. A hydroelectric project is under construction on the Yenisei River, near the village of Shushenskoye. The major part of work on the station has been completed in the 11th five-year plan period. Displayed in a stand is part of the ribbon which was cut at the unveiling ceremony for the first phase, commissioned ahead of schedule, of this 6.4mln kw station, the biggest in the world. Other exhibits in the stand include badges and special issues of the newspaper *Krasnoyarsky rabochi* (Krasnoyarsk Worker) printed to mark the occasion.

A number of exhibits serve as a reminder of the importance this country attaches to the development of the motor-industry. On view are two scale models of lorries: the 100-ton Kamaz-5320 made at the Kama Motorworks and the Belaz-75191 tip-up vehicle made at the Byelorussian Motorworks, one of the oldest in this country. At present, the Kama plant produces 150 thousand lorries a year.

Space-exhibits stand.

Occupying a central place in the exhibition is a large relief map illustrating the scale of the Soviet economy on which the Kama plant and other major projects of the twentieth century in European Russia, the Urals, Siberia, Central Asia and Kazakhstan are marked. Some of the projects will be of immense significance for the national economy. The dotted line at the bottom of the map is the 3,200-kilometre Baikal-Amur Railway. In terms of scale, technical complexity and the speed with which it has been constructed this project has no equals. Two-thirds of the line has been built over permafrost and more than 1,500 kilometres in highly seismic areas. The railway will play a key role in developing the productive forces of Siberia and the Far East.

On view is a memorial medal with the following wording, "From the Ye. O. Paton Electrical Welding Institute". The Paton Institute in Kiev invented a welding method which is widely used throughout this country.

In the left corner of the room furthest from the entrance is a desk souvenir shaped like a book. On one of its pages is Lenin's profile "drawn" by laser. This country is implementing a major complex programme on laser technologies. The laser with its wide-ranging applications will help to raise productivity to a significant extent. Another exhibit is a microminiature system, a robot consisting of 4,500 electronic components. The introduction of robots into industry opens up revolutionary possibilities for raising the efficiency of the entire Soviet economy.

This section also features memorial medals struck to commemorate the launching of the Earth's first man-made satellite—or Sputnik—on 4 October 1957, a number of photographs of Yuri Gagarin, the world's first man in space (1961), and a photograph, "Lenin in his Study in the Kremlin on 16 October 1918" which was taken into space on board the Voskhod spacecraft on 13 October, 1964. The photograph is signed by the cosmonauts, V. M. Komarov, K. P. Feoktistov, and B. B. Yegorov, who formed the crew. In the collection is a present from cosmonauts Yu. V. Malyshev and V. V. Aksyonov—a model of the Soyuz-T spacecraft.

The exhibition continues with a display of materials about efforts to translate into practice the provision from the CPSU Programme, "Everything for the sake of man, for the benefit of man." By 1985 social security benefits amounting to 138 thousand million roubles had been granted to Soviet citizens. By the end of the 11th five-year plan period, an average family of four will receive grants to the value of 2 thousand roubles. The state pays for free education and refresher courses. It also provides free medical aid, pensions, grants, scholarships, free and reduced-price accommodation at sanatoria and rest homes and maintains children at crèches and kindergartens.

Every day, nearly 30 thousand Soviet citizens move into new flats. Over slightly less than two months, enough flats are commissioned to populate a city of one million. A big photograph in the top tier of the display is of a new small town at the Baikal-Amur project. In accordance with the decrees of the Soviet Communist Party Congresses for the five-year plan, about 540 million square metres of housing is being built at the present time in the country. The Soviet Union is rightly called the land of new homes.

A table on display close by shows that more than four-fifths of the gainfully employed population have a higher or secondary education. In the 11th five-year plan period, the output of specialists with a higher or secondary education was ten million.

The programme for further improvements in standards of living embraces all aspects of life in this country. One of the priorities in this respect is improvement in the supply of foods to the population. An album (on display) called *The USSR Food Programme Over the Period Up to 1990* describes the specific measures taken to implement the Food Programme.

They anticipate completing the transfer of agriculture onto an industrial basis, extensive introduction of scientific methods of farming, intensification of agricultural production to achieve rational use of land, machinery, manpower, raw materials and financial resources. The USSR Food Programme envisages amalgamating the forces of the whole agro-industrial complex.

Industry keeps the villages supplied, particularly with deliveries of agricultural machinery. Models of the latest tractors are on view. Whereas in 1928, 27 thousand tractors and two combines were at work in our fields, today, in terms of total engine power, the USSR produces more tractors than any other country in the world, and, in terms of numbers, more than the USA, the FRG, France and Great Britain put together. Every day over 1,500 machines, destined to make work on the farm more efficient, come off the conveyor belt.

The display on the central wall is dedicated to the socialist emulation drive in which over one hundred million people are taking part. Some of the photographs in this section were taken at Communist *subbotniks* at the Moscow-Kazan Railway Yard. In 1919 workers at the yard set an example by repairing badly needed engines without asking for wages and in their own time. This was the first *subbotnik*: Lenin called their initiative "a great beginning". Today *subbotniks* are held all over the country to mark red-letter days in the history of the USSR.

A characteristic feature of socialism today is the close friendship that exists between the country's nations and nationalities. A special section is devoted to this theme. On view in a stand are the Order of Friendship Among Nations instituted by the Soviet government on 17 December 1972, emblems of the Soviet republics—forming part of the USSR and the texts of the CPSU Central Committee resolutions on the celebrations to mark the 50th and 60th anniversaries of the foundation of the Union. These rulings speak about the triumph of Lenin's national policies and outline ways of improving still further relations between nations and nationalities.

Developed socialism means government by the people, the broad involvement of workers in managing the affairs of society and state. One of the exhibits in a stand left of the map showing major Soviet projects for 1981-1985 is a page from Lenin's work, *The State and the Revolution* in which he writes that in contrast to the false and squalid democracy of the capitalist world, ... "Communism alone is capable of providing really complete democracy." Take the following example: more than half of the country's adult population—the working class, collective-farm peasantry, people's intelligentsia—took part in the discussion of the new edition of the Programme of the Communist Party of the Soviet Union, a major document containing the key to the country's further progress.

The last section of the exhibition is devoted to the CPSU's international politics. One of the exhibits is a photostat of a page from Lenin's "Theses for the Second Congress of the Communist International" in which he predicts a tendency "towards the creation of a single world economy, regulated by the proletariat of all nations as an integral whole and according to a common plan".

Some documents in the section show that Lenin's prediction has come true. In a special display is the Statute of the Council for Mutual Economic Assistance (CMEA) and CMEA's Comprehensive Programme for the further expansion and perfection of co-operation and development of socialist economic integration between the CMEA countries. Next to these documents are jointly devised five-year plans for co-operation in the economy, politics, and culture. The total population of the CMEA countries—Czechoslovakia, Bulgaria, Hungary, the German Democratic Republic, Cuba, Mongolia, Poland, Vietnam, Romania, and the Soviet Union—is nearly 450 million people. Diagrams show that over the more than thirty-five-year period since CMEA was founded, its members have nearly doubled their share of world production.

Co-operation based on Lenin's principles of socialist internationalism has assumed grandiose proportions. A photograph on display shows the laying of the Soyuz main gas pipeline and a medal, "For the Construction of the Soyuz Pipeline". It will be recalled that Soyuz has secured economic growth in several so-

Welding the final joint of the international gas pipeline at the Soviet-Czechoslovak frontier.

cialist countries, consolidated the fuel and energy supplies available to their economies and raised the efficiency of their industries. International projects like Soyuz promote progress and make the world socialist system more powerful.

Some materials in the section bear evidence to the efforts made by the CPSU and other Communist parties to unite the main motive forces of social development–world socialism, the working-class and communist movement, the peoples of states recently liberated from the colonial yoke, mass democratic movements–against imperialism and its policy of aggression and subjugation, in the name of democracy and social progress.

The Soviet Union and all the socialist countries lead the peace-loving forces of our planet. The Communist Party of the Soviet Union is putting into practice Lenin's behest (reproduced in large letters in the display): "To systematically promote a policy of peace, take all necessary steps to ensure its success".

And nearby is an excerpt from the present edition of the Programme of the Communist Party of the Soviet Union which speaks of the historical mission of socialism and of all the progressive, peace-loving forces of our planet to save humanity from catastrophe, to eliminate the nuclear arsenals. The might of the Soviet Union will always serve the cause of peace.

On stands and in display cases are copies of *Pravda* newspaper containing the Soviet Union's initiatives aimed at saving humanity from the threat of nuclear war, at freeing it from the burden of the arms race. Also to be seen here are a series of photographs illustrating the world-wide peace movement.

Room No. 23

THE COMMUNIST PARTY OF THE SOVIET UNION —THE LEADING FORCE IN SOVIET SOCIETY

In the first stand to the right of the entrance is the following prominently displayed quotation from Lenin's *The State and Revolution*,

"By educating the workers' party, Marxism educates the vanguard of the proletariat, capable of assuming power and *leading the whole people* to socialism, of directing and organising the new system, of being the teacher, the guide, the leader of all the working people".

Placed against a red background on the central wall of this small room is a photographic collage, "The Party Is the Mind, Honour and Conscience of Our Times." The title of the collage is based on a quotation from Lenin,

"We trust our Party. We see in it the mind, honour and conscience of our times", which conveys the theme of the collection in this room: that the CPSU's leading role is crucial for the economic, social and spiritual progress of Soviet society towards communism.

The exhibits include the present CPSU Programme adopted by the 27th Congress in 1986, verbatim reports of the 22nd to 27th Congresses, materials of the CPSU Central Committee plenums, and papers written by Communist Party leaders on issues relating to the construction of a new society. As a creatively developing doctrine, Marxism-Leninism ensures harmonious unity between revolutionary theory and revolutionary practice.

In the 83 years since it was established, the Communist Party of the Soviet Union has grown from a small organization into a powerful monolithic party of 19 million members. On a stand to the left as one enters the room is a chart which makes it clear that the Communist Party of the Soviet Union—having become the party of the whole people, the inspiring and organizing force behind the dynamic role of the masses as the makers of history—has not lost its class character: it remains the party of the working class.

The display is completed by a stand containing photographs of members of the Politbureau of the Central Committee of the Communist Party of the Soviet Union. Biographies of the Politbureau and candidate Politbureau members are given on a revolving stand.

The Communist Party is guided in all its activities by the well-tried Marxist-Leninist principles of proletarian, socialist internationalism, it steadily translates into life Lenin's style of work.

3

SECOND FLOOR

ROOMS NOS 24·34

(LENINIANA)

Lenin. A contemporary portrait by N. Andreyev.

SECOND-FLOOR ROOMS

Room devoted to the Ulyanovs.

The eleven rooms on the second floor accommodate exhibitions, some of them permanent. One of the rooms left of the escalator is dedicated to the Ulyanov family. Its collection includes documents, photographs, personal belongings and books from the Ulyanovs' library. It also has sculptured portraits of members of the family by M. Manizer, G. Lavrov, R. Larin, S. Loik, and M. Vertinskaya. The big photograph in the middle of the room is of the Ulyanovs in Simbirsk in 1879.

In some of the stands are items associated with Lenin's father, Ilya Nikolayevich, who worked selflessly to advance secondary education and to establish schools in villages. In his lifetime, Ilya Nikolayevich educated quite a few progressive-minded teachers who were proud to regard themselves as his followers.

There is a photostat copy of the certificate Ilya Ulyanov received on completing high school in Astrakhan and a diploma qualifying him as candidate of mathematics, given him in 1854 upon graduation from the department of physics and mathematics of Kazan University. There are also photographs associated with his life and work. Other exhibits are the maths and physics curricula for others, tact, will power and strength of character," recalled Lenin's younger brother Dmitri.

On exhibition are sheets of music which belonged to Lenin's mother, Maria Alexandrovna. They are evocative of evenings in Simbirsk when all the Ulyanov family gathered round the piano and listened to Maria Alexandrovna playing.

General view of Room No. 28.

Ilya Ulyanov drew up for his pupils and pages from his scientific papers. "He was the highest authority to us, a shining example of culture, erudition, industry, honesty and noble sentiments. We were also greatly influenced by our mother, Maria Alexandrovna who combined the best qualities of mother and teacher—boundless love for us, children, a vast intelligence, splendid organization, zest for life, consideration

There is a certificate with a gold medal of distinction awarded to Olga Ulyanova at the end of her studies at the Simbirsk Ladies Gymnasium in 1887. Displayed in another stand is a gymnasium essay written by Lenin's elder brother Alexander who was later executed for his part in an attempt on the Tsar's life. In answer to the question, "What qualities make one useful to society and to the state?" Alexander wrote, "In order to be a useful member of society a person must possess (a) honesty, (b) industriousness, (c) firm character, (d) intellect and (e) knowledge." Here also are pages from Alexander Ulyanov's paper on biology which won him a gold medal at St. Petersburg University. The example of his elder brother, his selflessness and readiness to sacrifice his life to free Russia from tyrants did a lot to influence Lenin's decision to become a revolutionary.

A number of documents reflect the life and work of Lenin's sisters Anna and Maria. They persevered with their revolutionary activities despite arrests, imprisonment and exile. Included in the exhibition are photographs of them taken at various times, their correspondence with Lenin, Maria's manuscripts, and some personal belongings, such as Maria's cloak. There are also a jacket, glasses, pen and briefcase, belonging to Dmitri Ulyanov who in 1903 attended the Second Congress of the RSDLP at which the revolutionary Marxist organizations in Russia were united into the Bolshevik Party. Subsequently, Dmitri Ulyanov, a doctor by profession, took part in the 1917 Revolution. He later held a number of Party and government posts. There are many photographs and documents relating to the life and work of Lenin's wife and comrade Nadezhda Krupskaya. These items testify to the invaluable help which Nadezhda Krupskaya gave Lenin throughout their married life. She was at his side at the most crucial points in his life. Together they went through the severe years of exile in Siberia and emigration. When they lived abroad, she set up Lenin's contacts with party organizations in Russia and was in charge of his correspondence. After the 1917 Revolution she was an official at the People's Commissariat of Education.

Krupskaya's works on teaching are displayed in the room. Her major research on the subject earned her a degree of Doctor of Pedagogical Science. She is the author of the most complete and detailed reminiscences about Lenin. Some of her personal effects are on view in show-cases—her cloak, desk set, a copy of her Party membership card and the medals she was awarded.

A permanent exhibition in a room to the right of the escalator is called, *"The Membership Cards of Lenin's Party"*. A table-stand in the middle of the room contains Xerox copies of a number of Lenin's personal Party membership cards. The first one of these is No. 527. It has yellowed with time. Card No. 114482 was issued to Lenin in 1922, while Card No. 00000001 issued in 1973 makes Lenin a permanent Party member. Placed next to this is a questionnaire filled in by Lenin on 17 September 1920 during the re-registration of members of the Moscow City Organization of the RCP(B).

One of the most important exhibitions on the second floor, is "V. I. Lenin and the Modern Revolutionary Movement". The documents on view in this room show Lenin to be a brilliant successor to Marx and Engels, an outstanding personality in the world Communist and working-class movement. There are also exhibits relating to the main forces in the revolutionary process today—the world socialist system, the anti-imperialist struggle of the working class and the upsurge of mass democratic movements in the non-socialist world, the struggle for the consolidation of their independence and social progress waged by countries which have thrown off the colonial yoke. The documents and materials also show the avant-garde role played by the international Communist movement.

The display opens with a bas-relief, "Karl Marx, Friedrich Engels and Vladimir Lenin", the three founders of Marxism-Leninism. In stands and show-cases arranged along the wall at the start of the exhibition are various editions of their works. These include *Selected Works* by K. Marx and F. Engels published in the language in which they originally appeared—German, French, etc.—a joint venture undertaken by the Marxism-Leninism Institutes at the CPSU Central Committee and the Central Committee of the Socialist Unity Party of Germany. Works by Lenin on view in stands and show-cases include: "What Is To Be Done?", "Two Tactics of Social-Democracy in the Democratic Revolution", *The State and the Revolution, "Left-Wing" Communism, An Infantile Disorder*. These works develop the doctrines on the Party, on the socialist revolution and dictatorship of the proletariat, and on the class allies of the proletariat in their struggle for democracy and socialism.

Among the exhibits are a number of unique mementoes of the workers' revolutionary struggle in various countries. On a stand at the start of the display is the rallying banner of the Paris Communards, presented to the workers of Moscow by the Communists of Paris in 1924. In 1871 this banner was hoisted by French workers over the barricades, the last defenders of the Commune gathered round it before their final struggle. On the same stand is the following quotation from Lenin,

"The cause of the Commune is the cause of the social revolution, the cause of the complete political and economic emancipation of the toilers. It is the cause of the proletariat of the whole world. And in this sense it is immortal."

It fell to the lot of Lenin and the Bolshevik Party to take up the cause of the Paris Commune, to prepare the ground for and lead the world's first socialist revolution, to unite the theory of scientific socialism with the broadest practical activities by the masses. To quote Lenin, the experience of the October Revolution and its main features "have a significance in the meaning of its effect on all the countries". This thesis is illustrated by materials on display in the first few sections of the room. In stands are photographs of the revolutionary developments which followed in the wake of the Russian Revolution in Germany, Slovakia, Hungary and other countries.

The table on the wall to the left of the entrance shows that over the period between 1917 and 1923, 43 Communist parties and groups were set up in different countries. Visitors to the room can see a documentary, *Under the Banner of Leninism*, about the development of the international revolutionary movement led by the Communists, and the emergence of the world socialist system. On one of the walls is a political map of the world, "Communist and Workers' Parties" which illustrates the scope of the present-day international Communist movement. The map confirms Lenin's words, "The Communist movement is growing splendidly throughout the world. It is ... broad, powerful, deep and invincible." Today there are Communist and workers' parties in almost one hundred countries. Among the exhibits are documents relating to the international Communist movement and photographs reflecting the main trends in co-operation between the Communist and workers' parties in their fight for peace, democracy and social progress.

A large section of the display in this part of the room is devoted to the strengthening of friendship and co-operation between countries of the socialist community united on the basis of Marxism-Leninism. The items on view include treaties of friendship and co-operation between the USSR and the fraternal socialist countries and various materials on co-ordination of efforts in the fight for peace, in developing the economies of the fraternal countries and in consolidating of their political union. This close co-operation is based on the alliance between Communist and workers' parties in the socialist countries. Exhibits relating to the alliance are as follows: documents issued by the Congresses held by fraternal parties, and photographs and materials of the Warsaw Treaty's Political Consultative Committee each of whose meetings is marked by new peace proposals put forward by the countries of the socialist community.

There are several exhibits referring to the development of socialist economic integration and to the Council for Mutual Economic Assistance (CMEA). There is a map of new projects in the CMEA countries and photographs of major joint ventures. These include Mir, a unified power system for the European socialist countries and the Soyuz international gas pipeline. Items displayed in the stands of this section include a memorial medal, "For the Construction of the Soyuz Gas Pipeline" and a steel worker's helmet autographed by workers from socialist countries, who took part in "Friendship", an international smelting ceremony in the town of Cherepovets in Northern Russia.

Statistics show that the CMEA countries, accounting for ten per cent of the world's total population, produce one-third of world industrial output and that they outstrip the capitalist countries in their rate of economic growth. Co-operation between socialist countries embraces an increasing number of areas. The visitors to this section may acquaint themselves with the all-embracing programme for the scientific-technical progress in the CMEA member-countries up to the year 2000.

On view is a marble sculpture presented to the CPSU Central Committee by the Soviet-Cuban cosmonaut team of Yuri Romanenko and A. Tamayo Méndez. Displayed next are pennants which were taken into space and signed by the Soviet and Romanian cosmonauts, Leonid Popov and Dumitru Prunariu and by the Soviet-Vietnamese cosmonaut team Viktor Gorbatko and Pham Tuan. A miniature book on display, *The Internationale*, was a space companion for the Hungarian cosmonaut Bertalan Farkas. There are also postcards bearing the autographs of the Soviet and Polish cosmonauts, Pyotr Klimuk and Miroslaw Hermaszewski.

Exhibits in the room show that the community of socialist countries is the most dynamic economic and political force in the world today, the mainstay of peace and security.

The items displayed on the wall to the right of the entrance illustrate the working-class anti-imperialist struggle at the present time. Included in the exhibition is a short documentary, *The Class Battles in the Capitalist Countries*. There are numerous photographs of protest demonstrations in the capitalist countries against unemployment, political reprisals, and the aggressive plans devised by imperialism. Statistics testify to the growing military budgets of NATO and the United States. Other photographs expose imperialism: they show the towns and villages of the Lebanon, Beirut reduced to rubble after the Israeli raids, Palestinian villagers whose homes were destroyed by the Israelis, the armed seizure of Grenada and the aggressive operations against Nicaragua, and the peaceful civilians of Ulster on whom the British soldiers train their guns. Yet no force in the world can stop the revolutionary process or reverse the course of history.

The anti-imperialist struggle of Asian, African and Latin American countries who have won their liberation is living testimony to the triumph of Lenin's ideas. Many newly-independent states espouse Marxism-Leninism and benefit from the experience of real socialism. Photographs and documents in this part of the display illustrate the assistance these new states receive from the Soviet Union and other socialist countries. These exhibits testify to the fair and equitable relations existing between these two groups of states.

Another section is devoted to the Leninist foreign policies pursued by the CPSU and the Soviet state, and to the efforts they make to unite all peace forces of the world. The collection in this part of the room features the Decree on Peace, the first law to be proclaimed by the new Soviet government in 1917. It is displayed side by side with materials of the 25th, 26th and 27th Congresses of the CPSU which outline a world-wide campaign for the preservation of peace. There are photographs of peace rallies and marches staged by Soviet workers in support of this country's peace initiatives. The CPSU and the Soviet government are active in their efforts to carry out Lenin's behest "to continue this peace policy systematically, taking all appropriate measures to ensure its success".

Lenin's name is dear to all the progressive workers of the world. There are a series of exhibitions on this theme in the rooms to the left of the escalator. The exhibits include memorial medals, pictures, woven, embroidered and tapestry portraits of Lenin made in the GDR and Hungary, Bulgaria and Czechoslovakia, Vietnam and Mongolia, in Italy, France and Argentina, in Mexico, Japan, Afghanistan, and in many other countries.

A permanent display, *"Presents to V. I. Lenin from the Working People"*, contains some unique items. The following modest presents—a 1920 model of an electric insulator, a mechanical calculating machine of 1920, and a brick of peat from a peat field of the early 20s—are mementoes from the early history of Soviet power when every step towards economic recovery was incredibly difficult. Other items include albums of photographs presented by factory workers, procelain plates, vases and bowls with dedicatory inscriptions from the workers of an old Russian Porcelain Factory in Dulyovo, near Moscow. Visitors tend to spend a long time in this room, lingering over the exhibits which are a vivid evocation of the age. A portrait of Lenin done on a lotus leaf from India, invariably attracts interest.

There have been many exhibitions of pictures dedicated to Lenin in the second-floor rooms, featuring paintings by the Soviet artists I. Brodsky, A. Gerasimov, V. Serov, Ye. Kibrik, N. Zhukov, and P. Vasiliev. On display here are works by the Soviet artist and sculptor N. Andreyev, one of the few for whom Lenin sat.

One of the permanent displays on the second floor is *"Lenin in the Amateur Arts and Crafts"*. It features carpets, suzané[1] and mosaic compositions on the subject of Lenin. Here are also portraits of Lenin done in silk, wool, feathers, straw, and other materials by skilled craftsmen from Azerbaijan, Armenia, the Russian Federation, Kazakhstan, Uzbekistan, the Ukraine, Byelorussia and the other constituent republics. There are constant additions to the display, as new generations of Soviet artists and craftsmen continue to dedicate their works to Lenin, their source of inspiration.

The artistic Leniniana continues with the *display, "Lenin in the Cinema and Theatre"*. Stills from documentaries arranged along the top of the walls of the room show Lenin at festive demonstrations in Red Square, in his Kremlin study, at Comintern Congresses, and at mass rallies of workers and peasants.

---

[1] A rectangular piece of cotton or silk cloth embroidered in different patterns. It is used as a wall decoration by the Uzbeks and Tajiks.

Main staircase to the first floor.

Entrance hall of the museum.

Part of Vladimir's room at his parents' home in Simbirsk (now the Lenin House-Museum).

General view of Room No. 9 devoted to preparations for the October armed uprising.

Room No. 15

First-floor corridor.

"As a current of political thought and as a political party, Bolshevism has existed since 1903." This quote from Lenin forms the theme of the exhibition in Room No. 3

S. Lukin, *It Has Come True at Last.*

L. Shmatko, *Lenin standing before a map of the electrification of Russia. The Eighth All-Russia Congress of Soviets. December 1920.*

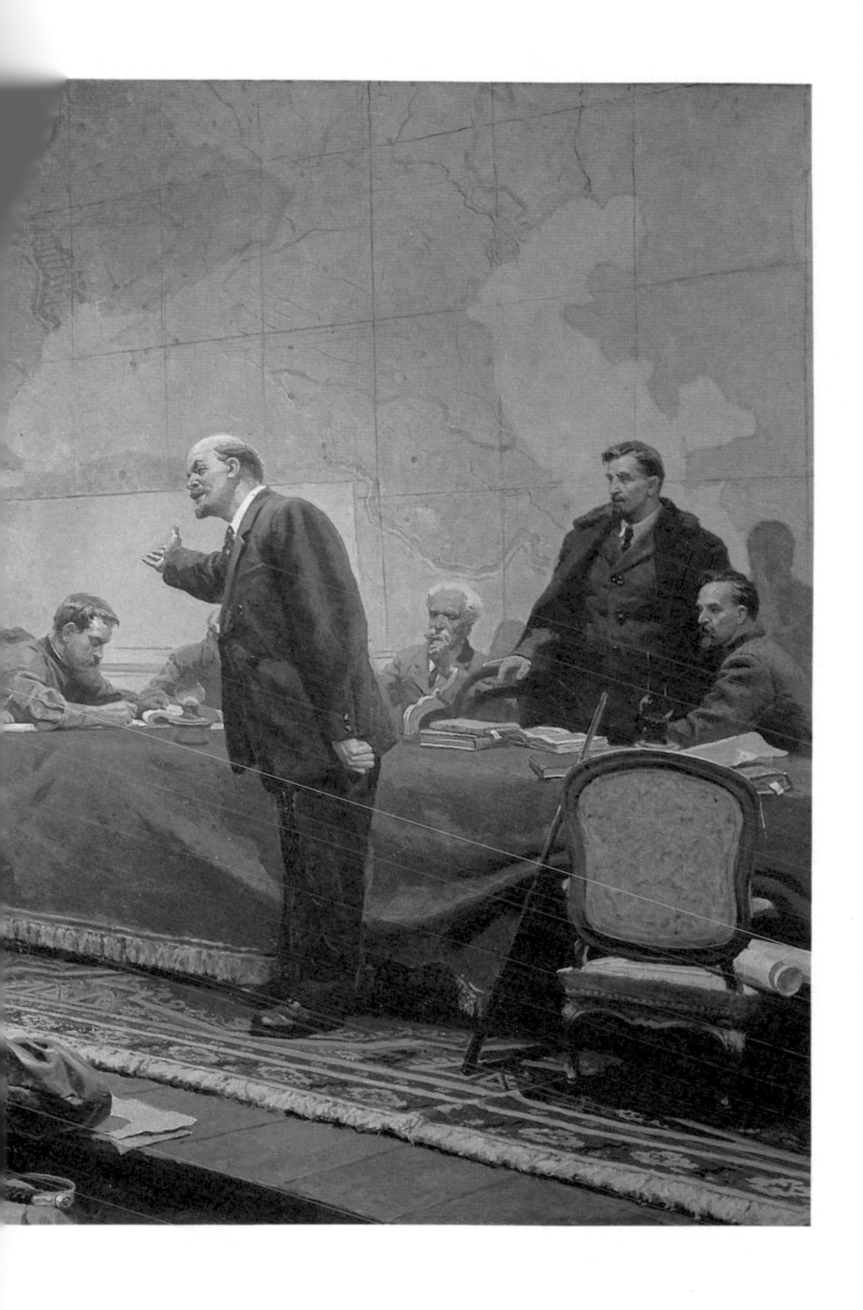

V. Serov, *Village Messengers Come to Lenin.*

Lenin's study in the Kremlin. (A reconstruction.)

General view of Room No. 28.

The exhibits in Room No. 19 are devoted to Lenin's works.

Scale model of the Kamaz-5320 truck with a load capacity of over one hundred tons (the Kama Motorworks)

Scale model of the Belaz-75191 heavy-duty dump truck manufactured by the Byelorussian Motorworks.

Decorative vase and plate, donated to the museum by craftsmen from the village of Kubachi, north-eastern Caucasus.

Mosaic portrait of Lenin (first floor).

Kerchief that belonged to Edmond Devaux, a French Communist shot by the Nazis during the Second World War.

Moscow. Red Square.

Lenin is the subject of many films and plays. Visitors to the room can see fragments from feature films on the Russian revolutionary leader which have become Soviet classics. There are photographs of scenes from plays, with actors like M. Shtraukh and B. Shchukin playing the part of Lenin. Other exhibits in this section are models of stage sets for plays and theatrical productions about Lenin, and playbills.

To commemorate the leader of the international proletariat, plaques have been installed on the houses where Lenin lived and worked, while streets in many cities have been named after him. Lenin Museums, Memorial Houses and Museum Flats have been set up in many foreign countries. Such is the theme of the exhibition: *"The Lenin Memorial Places"* in the next room. It includes 350 documentary photographs and an electrified map in the middle of the room indicating the places where Lenin lived and worked. Visitors can see a documentary film plus slides about the countries and cities where he stayed.

The passages between the rooms on the second floor are used for temporary exhibitions of posters dedicated to Lenin.

Practical Information

The Central Lenin Museum in Moscow (2 Ploshchad Revolutsii) is open daily except Mondays between 11 a.m. and 7.30 p.m. in winter, and 10 a.m. to 6.30 p.m. in summer. Admission is free.

Guided tours can be arranged by phoning the Excursion Bureau: 925-48-08

The nearest Metro Station is "Ploshchad Revolutsii". Buses Nos. 3, 5 and 111 stop outside the Museum.

Apart from guided tours, the Museum organizes specialist and general lectures, film shows and readings on Lenin, conferences, and meetings with Party and labour veterans.

Lenin Museums in the Soviet Union

There are some five hundred places linked with Lenin's name in this country. Many of these have memorial plaques. The museums marked by an asterisk in the list below are regarded as memorial.

Baku	123a Prospekt Neftyanikov
Kazan and region	(a) 58 Ulitsa Ulyanovykh* (b) Kazan University*, 18 Ulitsa Lenina (c) the village of Lenino-Kokushkino* (outside the city)
Kiev	2 Ulitsa Kreshchatik
Krasnoyarsk	(a) 27 Ulitsa Markovskogo* (b) 2 Ulitsa Melkombinatskaya* (c) The Svyatoi Nikolai Steamer-Museum*, off Ulitsa Dubrovinskogo and Ulitsa Surikova
Krasnoyarsk territory	State Memorial Museum Preserve, "Lenin's Siberian exile", the village of Shushenskoye* there is a branch of the Museum in the village of Yermakovskoye at 15 Ulitsa Marksa*
Leningrad	(a) 5/1 Ulitsa Khalturina*

	(b) Flat 13, 7 Pereulok Ilyicha* (c) Flat 24, 52 Ulitsa Lenina* (d) Flat 20, 17 Desyataya Sovietskaya Ulitsa* (e) Flat 180, 1 Serdobolskaya Ulitsa* (f) Flat 31, 32 Naberezhnaya Reki Karpovki* (g) Flat 9, 5 Khersonskaya Ulitsa* (h) Smolny*, Ploshchad Proletarskoi Diktatury*
Leningrad region	(a) Razliv Railway Station, 3 Ulitsa Yemelyanova* (b) Tarkhovka Railway Station* (c) Ilyichovo* (d) Vyborg, 15 Rubezhnaya Ulitsa*
Lvov	20 Prospekt Lenina
Moscow	(a) 2 Ploshchad Revolutsii (b) 1 Ploshchad Lenina (c) V. I. Lenin Flat and Study in the Kremlin* (d) Flats 13-14, 9 Manezhnaya Ulitsa*
Moscow region	(a) Gorki Leninskiye* (b) Kaliningrad, 1 Ulitsa Ilyicha* (c) Podolsk, 47 Prospekt Lenina*
Pskov	(a) 3 Ulitsa Lenina* (b) 5 Pereulok *Iskry**
Riga	17 Ulitsa Cēsu Flat 5, 18 Ulitsa Kirova*
Tashkent	30 Prospekt Lenina

Tbilisi	29 Prospekt Rustaveli
Ulyanovsk	(a) 58 Ploshchad Stoletiya so Dnya Rozhdeniya V. I. Lenina* (b) 58 Ulitsa Lenina*
Ufa	78 Ulitsa Dostoyevskogo*
Frunze	Ploshchad Ala-Too

* * *

One can learn more about Lenin's life and work at the memorial museums dedicated to the Ulyanov family in Astrakhan, Vologda and region, Kiev and Penza.

Lenin Museums Abroad

German Democratic Republic:

Leipzig	(a) 48 Russenstrasse*
	(b) 19/21 Rosa Luxemburg Strasse
Berlin	8 Unter der Linden

Mongolian People's Republic:

Ulan Bator	Ploshchad Sukhe-Bator

Poland:

Warsaw	62 al. Gen. K. Swerczewskiego
Craców	(a) 5 Ul. Topolowa
	(b) 41 Ul. Krolowej Jadwigi*
Poronin	160 Ul. Lenina*
Bialy Dunajec	6 Ul. Lenina*
Nowy Targ	10 Harzerska*

Czechoslovakia:

Prague	7 Hybernska
Bratislava	26 Obrancov mieru

Finland:

Helsinki	1 Sornaisten Rantatie, Apt. 22
Tampere	19 Hallitaskatu

France:

Paris	4 Marie-Rose*

Notes

p. 19

The Liberal Populists were members of a liberation movement in the second half of the past century in Russia. They were Utopian socialists who favoured peaceful socio-political reform.

p. 19

The Legal Marxists represented an ideological and political trend among the Russian middle-of-the-road intellectuals who in the 1890s sought to replace Marxism with a liberal theory for reforming capitalist society. They campaigned for bourgeois-democratic liberties. By the end of the 1900s their views had become purely liberal. They were known as "legal" because they wrote for legal magazines like *Novoye slovo*, *Zhizn*, etc.

p. 22

At different stages since its foundation in 1898, the Communist Party of the Soviet Union has had different names:

between 1898 and 1917 it was known as the RSDLP, the Russian Social-Democratic Labour Party;

between 1917 and 1918 it became the RSDLP(B), or the Russian Social-Democratic Labour Party of the Bolsheviks to distinguish its members from the Mensheviks, also Social-Democrats;

between 1918 and 1925 it was the RCP(B), the Russian Communist Party (Bolshevik);

between 1925 and 1952 it was re-named the All-Union Communist Party (Bolshevik). It was given its present name at the 19th Congress in 1952.

p. 23

The Economists were champions of an opportunistic trend among the Russian Social-Democrats at the turn of the century. Maintaining that the political struggle was a prerogative of the capitalist class, they insisted that the working class should pursue purely economic goals. They played down the importance of the revolutionary theory, and in Russia they opposed the efforts to set up a nation-wide proletarian party.

p. 27

The Socialist Revolutionaries were members of the biggest petty-bourgeois party in Russia in 1901-1923 who upheld the interests of petty capitalists in the town and countryside. The Party evolved from petty-bourgeois revolutionary sentiments to an alliance with the counter-revolutionaries. After the 1917 Revolution, the Socialist Revolutionaries engineered a number of counter-revolutionary revolts. By 1923 their party had fallen apart.

p. 30

The Centrists represented an ideological and political tendency which arose out of the battle between reformist and revolutionary trends within the Second International. The Centrists wanted to iron out the essentially irreconcilable differences between the two trends by making concessions to the reformists on key issues of theory and tactics in the working-class movement. Trotskyism in Russia was a variety of Centrism.

p. 43

The Second International was an association of socialist parties. It was set up in 1889 with Friedrich Engels as one of the founders. At the turn of the century it was taken over by Right-wing opportunistic elements who were opposed by the revolutionary trend, the main force in which was the Bolshevik Party led by Lenin. The revolutionary Marxist-Leninist parties which emerged following the 1917 Revolution in Russia set up the Third Communist International.

p. 47

Austria-Hungary was a dual monarchy (1867-1918) established as a result of the transformation of the Habsburg Empire on the basis of an agreement between the ruling classes of Austria and Hungary. The two parts of the Empire became sovereign entities. The collapse of the Empire in 1918 led to the establishment of Austria, Hungary, and Czechoslovakia, with parts of Austria-Hungary ceded to Yugoslavia, Romania, Poland, and Italy.

p. 48

The State Duma was a representative law-drafting body in the Russian Empire between 1906 and 1917. It examined various legislative proposals which were then debated by the State Council and endorsed by the Tsar. Four Dumas were elected.

p. 59

Inessa Armand (1874-1920) was a Bolshevik leader in the Russian and international revolutionary movement. From 1904 she represented the Bolshevik Party at international socialist conferences. She also taught at the Party School in Longjumeau. Following the 1917 Revolution she was in charge of the Women's Section of the Party's Central Committee.

p. 60

The Provisional Government was the central body of capitalists and landlord power in Russia set up after the February 1917 Revolution. It continued the unpopular imperialist war and suppressed the revolutionary movement. It was toppled in the October Revolution of 1917.

p. 61

Dual power: was the peculiar situation existing in Russia after the 1917 February Revolution when power was shared by the capitalist Provisional Government and the Soviets, acting in the interests of the revolutionary democrats. Dominated by the petty-bourgeois parties, the Soviets ceded their share of power to the Provisional Government in July 1917, after the latter had ordered to shoot down peaceful demonstrating workers in Petrograd. This event marks the end of dual power in Russia and the peaceful period of the Revolution.

p. 61

Kollontai Alexandra Mikhailovna (1872-1952) was a Soviet Party and government leader who took part in the 1917 Revolution. In 1920 she became head of the Women's Section at the Party's Central Committee. Between 1923 and 1945 she was Soviet political representative, commercial representative and ambassador in Norway and Sweden.

p. 65

The Putilov Works, founded in 1801, was one of the oldest steel mills in St. Petersburg. Known today as the Kirovsky Zavod association, it produces tractors, engines for ocean-going ships, steel and rolled metal.

p. 67

Officer cadets were students of military academies in Russia.

p. 73

The Smolny Institute is a historical and architectural monument in Leningrad. It was built in the 19th century as an institute for the education of the daughters of noblemen. In the days before and after the armed uprising in October 1917, Smolny, which accommodated the Petrograd Soviet and the Military Revolutionary Council, was the headquarters of the revolutionary forces. Before 10 March 1918 it was the seat of the Soviet government–the Council of People's Commissars (Sovnarkom).

p. 80

"The Left Communists" were a group within the Bolshevik Party who were opposed to the Brest-Litovsk Peace Treaty and in favour of a continuation of the revolutionary war.

p. 82

The workers' faculties were general educational departments (set up between 1919 and 1940) for young workers without secondary education to prepare them to go to college. They were attached to colleges and universities and gave classes after working hours.

p. 82

RSFSR, the Russian Soviet Federative Socialist Republic, was the first Soviet republic proclaimed on 25 October 1917.

p. 83

Fotiyeva Lidiya Alexandrovna (1881-1975) was an active member of the Russian revolutionary movement. She took part in three Russian revolutions, having joined the Bolsheviks in 1904. From 1918 to 1930 she held secretarial posts at the Sovnarkom and at the Council of Labour and Defence (See Notes to p. 104). She is mostly remembered as Lenin's personal secretary from 1918 till his death in 1924. She later became staff member of the Lenin Museum in Moscow.

p. 86

The Entente, an imperialist bloc consisting of Britain, France and Russia, was formed in 1904-1907. During World War I it was joined by another twenty or so countries. The failure of the anti-Soviet intervention and the split between its members led to its collapse.

p. 90

Communist subbotniks are days of unpaid voluntary work done by Soviet citizens for the benefit of society. The first *subbotnik* was held in 1919 at the Moscow branch of the Kazan Railway. Lenin described the first *subbotnik* as a "great beginning". *Subbotniks* are mainly organized at weekends, hence their name from the Russian word *subbota*, Saturday.

p. 96

Khalturin Stepan Nikolayevich (1856-1882), one of the first revolutionary workers, organized "The Northern Union of the Russian Workers". In 1880 he was responsible for a bomb attack at the Tsar's residence, the Winter Palace in St. Petersburg. He was hanged in Odessa for his part in the murder of the Odessa Military District Prosecutor notorious for his brutality.

p. 98

VTsIK, the All-Russia Central Executive Council, was the supreme legislative, executive and controlling agency of state power in the RSFSR, in 1917-1937.

p. 98

The All-Russia Congress of Soviets, was the supreme body of power in the RSFSR between 1918 and 1922. From the establishment of the USSR in December 1922 until 1936 it was known as the All-Union Congress of Soviets. At present, the supreme power in this country is vested in the USSR Supreme Soviet.

p. 99

Grain requisitioning was a system for the procurement of agricultural produce in Soviet Russia in 1919-1921, an element of "military Communism" policies. In those years the peasants undertook to supply the state with all surplus grain they had at firm prices, keeping for themselves only what had been established as absolutely necessary for their personal and farming needs. In 1921 this system was replaced with a tax in kind.

p. 104

The Council of Labour and Defence was the body in the Soviet state responsible for the economy and defence. It was appointed by the Council of People's Commissars (Sovnarkom) as one of its commissions.

p. 104

The Narrow Council of People's Commissars was a permanent commission at the RSFSR Sovnarkom in 1918-1930. In order to save time its meetings were used for preliminary debates on issues due to be decided by the full Sovnarkom. The Narrow Council also decided certain economic and financial matters.

p. 104

The Revolutionary Committees were ad hoc emergency agencies of Soviet power set up during the Civil War of 1918-1920 throughout the country. Since the political situation in the country was grave, the Revolutionary Committees assumed all civilian and military powers.

p. 106

Treaties ... concluded with Estonia, Latvia and Lithuania ... early in the 1920s. Soviet power was installed in the three Baltic republics, which had been part of the Russian Empire, immediately after the October Revolution. However, all three republics were taken over by capitalist regimes which concluded treaties with the RSFSR. In 1940, Estonia, Latvia and Lithuania became constituent republics of the Soviet Union.

Moscow
Centre of the City

1. Museum of the Revolution
2. Monument to Alexander Pushkin
3. Stanislavsky and Nemirovich-Danchenko Opera and Ballet Theatre
4. Nikolai Ostrovsky Flat-Museum
5. Tsentralnaya Hotel
6. Moscow City Council of People's Deputies
7. Monument to Yuri Dolgoruky, Founder of Moscow
8. Moscow Art Theatre
9. Budapest Hotel
10. Central Department Store (TsUM)
11. Children's World Store—Detsky Mir
12. Berlin Hotel
13. Maly Theatre of the USSR A. Ostrovsky Monument
14. Monument to Karl Marx
15. Bolshoi Theatre of the USSR
16. Mayakovsky Flat-Museum
17. Politechnical Museum
18. Metropol Hotel
19. State Department Store (GUM)
20. Museum of History and Reconstruction of Moscow
21. Moskva Hotel
22. Intourist Hotel
23. National Hotel

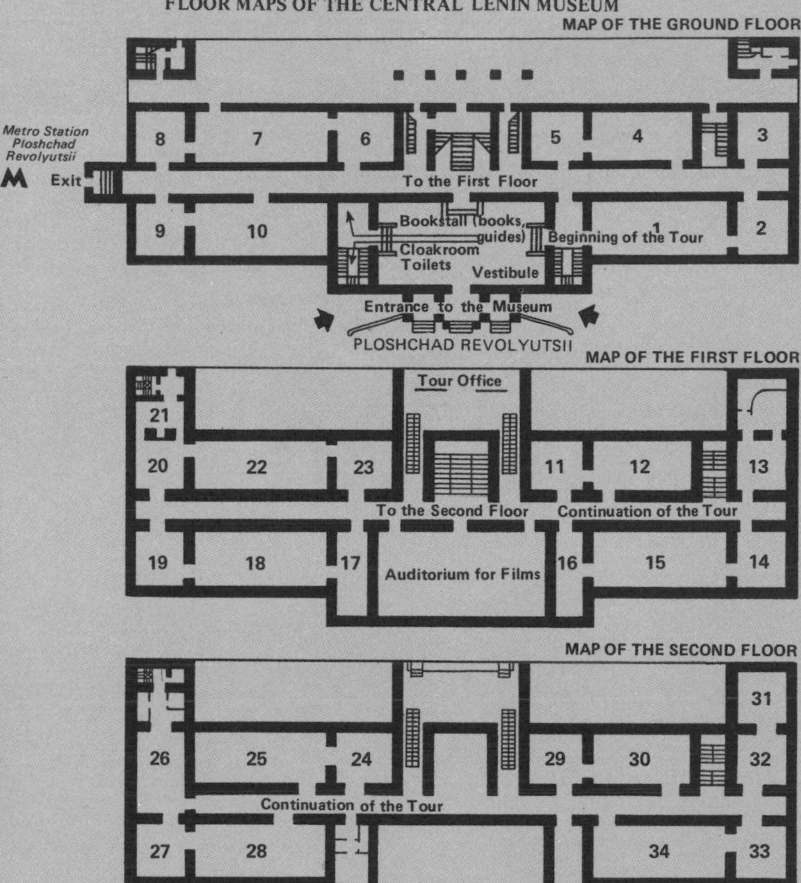

24. Moscow State University (old buildings)
25. Historical Museum
26. Tchaikovsky's Statue near the Conservatoire
27. House of Friendship with Foreign Countries
28. Central Exhibition Hall
29. Lenin Mausoleum
30. Lenin Monument in the Kremlin
31. St. Basil's Cathedral (Cathedral of the Intercession)
32. Rossia Hotel. Central Concert Hall
33. Bucharest Hotel
34. State Lenin Library
35. Marx and Engels Museum
36. Pushkin Museum of Fine Arts

REQUEST TO READERS

Raduga Publishers would be glad to have your opinion of this book, its translation and design and any suggestions you may have for future publications.

Please send all your comments to 17, Zubovsky Boulevard, Moscow, USSR.

ИБ № 2389

Редактор русского текста М. М. Державина
Контрольный редактор А. В. Буяновская
Художник И. П. Маркарова
Художественный редактор Н. Н. Щербакова
Технические редакторы И. К. Дергунова, Г. И. Немтинова

Сдано в набор 30.08.85. Подписано в печать 12.06.86. Формат 84 × 108⅓₂. Бумага офсетная. Гарнитура максима. Печать офсетная. Условн. печ. л. 9,24. Усл. кр. отт. 20,80. Уч. изд. л. 11,70. Тираж 11890 экз. Заказ № 05657. Цена 1 р. 40 к. Изд. № 2375

Издательство „Радуга" Государственного комитета СССР по делам издательств, полиграфии и книжной торговли.
Москва, 119859, Зубовский бульвар, 17
Изготовлено в ГДР

Places where V.I. Lenin lived, worked or came to visit

V.I. Lenin state museums, memorial houses and apartments